'*Class Action* is a vivid, honest and compelling account of a difficult life lived on the Cape Flats during the apartheid years. What the author does better than most is to offer an interwoven account of the personal and the social in ways that helps us understand both better – how apartheid not only crushed black lives but at the same time emboldened the resistance against this crime against humanity. From the ashes of a broken life, Charles Abrahams rises to lead on a world stage the first class-action lawsuit on behalf of victims of apartheid. Nobody has told the story of our violent past with such a clear sense of the present and such a hopeful vision of the future.'

– Jonathan Jansen

CLASS ACTION

CLASS ACTION

In pursuit of a larger life

CHARLES ABRAHAMS

PENGUIN BOOKS

Published by Penguin Books
an imprint of Penguin Random House South Africa (Pty) Ltd
Reg. No. 1953/000441/07
The Estuaries No. 4, Oxbow Crescent, Century Avenue, Century City, 7441
PO Box 1144, Cape Town, 8000, South Africa
www.penguinrandomhouse.co.za

Penguin
Random House
South Africa

First published 2019

1 3 5 7 9 10 8 6 4 2

Publication © Penguin Random House 2019
Text © Charles Abrahams 2019

Cover photographs © Lindsey Appolis (top) and Greg Nicolson (bottom)

PUBLISHER: Marlene Fryer
MANAGING EDITOR: Robert Plummer
EDITOR: Lauren Smith
PROOFREADER: Bronwen Maynier
COVER DESIGNER: Monique Cleghorn
TEXT DESIGNER: Ryan Africa
TYPESETTER: Monique van den Berg

Set in 11.5 pt on 15 pt Minion

Printed by **novus print**, a Novus Holdings company

MIX
Paper from
responsible sources
FSC
www.fsc.org   FSC® C022948

ISBN 978 1 77609 352 6 (print)
ISBN 978 1 77609 353 3 (ePub)

Disclaimer: Some events and dialogues have been compressed. Certain names have
been changed to protect the privacy of the individuals involved. The author has done
his best to ensure that the events in this book are as truthful as he knows them to be.

In memory of my late mother, Kathleen Abrahams

Contents

'The unexamined life is not worth living.' – Socrates

—⚊—

'The examined life is painful.' – Cornell West

Preface

I first encountered the term 'class action' as a first-year law student in 1987, when I heard about *Brown* v *Board of Education*, a famous 1950s US Supreme Court case concerning racially segregated schooling. A group of African American parents had taken several US states to court for refusing to educate black children in the same schools as whites, arguing that this violated the US constitution's Fourteenth Amendment, which provides for equal protection before the law.

South Africa was still in the grip of apartheid's racially divided education system, and I feared being the only student who hadn't read about the case. I wasn't interested in the fact that it was a class action, but the court's decision was important to me. The parents had won the case because it was ruled that separating black children from their peers would generate a feeling of inferiority that might never be undone.

The judgment provided a grim view of the effects of race-based education. I, too, had been educated along racial lines and knew exactly what that sense of inferiority felt like.

In the mid-1990s, news of tobacco class actions in the US occasionally featured in the media and I started to pay attention to the concept of a class action itself. It amazed me that one or a few people could claim millions of dollars against tobacco companies, something unheard of in South African law. My intuitive response was to think of the claimants as smoking addicts with illnesses so severe that it warranted huge pay-outs from the tobacco companies, for selling hazardous products without the appropriate warnings. Only after further enquiry did I realise that it had to do with class action. Like the parents in *Brown* v *Board of Education*, the smokers not only filed the lawsuits on their own behalf, but also on behalf of other ill smokers. It started to make sense.

Class actions are designed to accommodate groups of people – i.e. classes – affected by the same set of facts, circumstances and laws. For instance, if tobacco companies know that smoking is harmful and fail to warn people thereof, smokers who fall ill may institute civil claims against the companies for damages. Instead of each smoker filing his or her own lawsuit, one or a few smokers can do so and a successful result can benefit all those who fall into the same class (i.e. those with smoking-related illnesses). It makes economic sense, and allows people who may not have the means to pursue a lawsuit to know justice. Class action is legally efficient in the same manner that retail wholesalers who provide discounts on bulk purchases are economically efficient for their customers. Thus, class actions are like the retail wholesalers of law.

By 1999, a series of Holocaust lawsuits had cemented my interest in class actions. In New York, Holocaust survivors sued Swiss banks for knowingly retaining and concealing assets of victims and their heirs, often preventing access through prohibitive requirements for proof of ownership. I didn't know much about the law used to bring the cases, but I was struck by stories of the survivors recounted in the suits. One story was of Gizella Weisshaus, a Romanian Jew who was only fourteen years old when her family was gassed at Auschwitz. She was forced into slave labour, and liberated by the Russians a year later, at the end of the war. In the 1950s, she began approaching Swiss banks in an attempt to recover money her father had saved there to keep it hidden from the Nazis. Because she did not have an account number, however, the banks would not help her. In 1996, half a century after Auschwitz, she sued the banks for failing to return money and valuables deposited by Holocaust victims. Soon after, thousands came forward to join the case with their own stories and claims that had been silenced or ignored.

I was impressed by the might of class action and realised I'd stumbled upon a powerful weapon for righting socio-political wrongs. The lawsuits also ignited a spark in me about our own painful past under apartheid: if Holocaust survivors could tell their stories through class action, why couldn't black South Africans do the same?

In 2002, I partnered with seasoned US class-action lawyer Michael Hausfeld to file a lawsuit in New York on behalf of apartheid survivors, ordinary men and women who bore the brunt of the regime's worst excesses – torture, rape, murder and other gross human-rights violations at the hands of security forces. The suit targeted several multinational banks and corporations that supported the apartheid government with arms and ammunition, and military transport and technology. Though their circumstances differed, the claimants' stories were as horrifying as those of the holocaust survivors'.

For fifteen years, as Michael and I litigated the case in New York, my own story began to take shape. I drew inspiration from my clients' stories and the more I immersed myself in their suffering, the deeper I was able to dig into my own life under apartheid, a system designed to divide people not only by race, but also by class. My story began on the Cape Flats where I was born in abject poverty and designated 'coloured', South Africa's unique subclass of black African. Like most black South Africans, my life's journey began far behind those in the white class, hamstrung by social ills, with obstacles at every turn. In my scramble to move forward, I saw apartheid stripped of all its pretences: the coloured ghettos on the Cape Flats; the crippling poverty; the way family and social life crumbled under domestic violence; the young men engaged in lethal gang war; and the cruel corporal punishment teachers used as if it were a pastime. Apartheid, in its naked reality, was about systematically stripping us of the last human defence – dignity. That was the story of my childhood. The story of *Class Action* is an act of taking my dignity back.

1

I would have been world famous

At age twelve, I was well on my way to becoming the world's next famous heart surgeon. I had everything going for me; it was only a matter of time.

I'd been inspired a few years earlier, when my mother told me the story of Dr Chris Barnard performing the world's first heart transplant at Groote Schuur Hospital in Cape Town. I was so fascinated that I'd vowed to one day be a world-famous heart surgeon too.

Then our class teacher, Mr Hendricks, told us that the school inspector would be coming to visit and that each of us had to tell him what we wanted to be when we grew up. For days I waited for this opportunity, and on the morning in question I was riveted with excitement. Most kids who got up before me said they wanted to be teachers, traffic cops or policemen, sticking to a short list of options.

When it was my turn, I stood up from my bench and tucked my scruffy little blue shirt into my oversized grey shorts, fastened by a large silver nappy pin. I smiled broadly. 'Meneer! Ek wil 'n hartchirurg word.' (Sir! I want to become a heart surgeon.)

The classroom fell silent and the school inspector's friendly, smiling face took on a puzzled frown. I looked around, wondering if I'd said something wrong. Somewhat hesitantly, the school inspector politely asked me to repeat what I'd said. This time, I spoke as loudly as possible, so that no one in the room would miss a word. 'Meneer! Ek wil 'n hartchirurg word!'

In almost total unison, the entire class burst into hysterical laughter. I looked around, dumbfounded. My classmates were laughing their guts out. I turned anxiously to the inspector and Mr Hendricks, who were at the front of the class. They too were laughing. The inspector adjusted his big, round glasses as he struggled to regain his composure. Mr Hendricks's hunchback bounced to the rhythm of his giggles.

Eventually, the inspector walked over to me and silenced the class. He looked me up and down. 'Seun,' he asked in a calm, collected voice, 'van waar is jy?' (Boy, where are you from?)

My heart pummelled my chest. I wriggled my fingers and looked around the classroom before I answered, 'Nooitgedacht, meneer.'

'Waar in Nooitgedacht?' (Where in Nooitgedacht?)

'… Bream Way, meneer.'

Again, the class burst out laughing. Almost everyone knew Bream Way to be the poorest, most violent street in Nooitgedacht. Kids were shy to say they were from Bream Way for fear of being ridiculed. From the disdainful way the inspector looked at my scruffy shirt, tattered shoes and nappy pin, it felt as if he'd already known I was from Bream Way.

With a broad smile and self-assured tone, he said, 'Seun, dankie dat jy dit met ons gedeel het, maar miskien moet jy nie so hoog mik nie.' (Boy, thank you for sharing that with us, but perhaps you should not aim too high.)

His comment promptly elicited another outburst of laughter. Speechless, I sat down, feeling terrible. I tried to put on a brave face as some boys quietly poked fun at me: 'Boy, perhaps you should not aim too high.'

The inspector continued asking the class what futures they anticipated. John 'Langkop' (Longhead) said he wanted to be a mechanic. Shireen, one of Mr Hendricks's chosen, who sat at the front of the class, wanted to be a teacher. And so it went on: traffic officers, firemen, truck drivers, teachers, nurses, policemen. As I sat there, listening to each one of them, I cursed myself for having been so stupid as to think that I could be a heart surgeon.

At home that afternoon, I was too embarrassed to tell my mother what had happened. I moped, feeling miserable. All I wanted was to get the inspector's comments and the laughter out of my head. In the days that followed, many of my classmates continued to tease me and I wished I didn't have to be at school. I was angry with them, but angrier with the school inspector and Mr Hendricks. I'd thought that teachers were always right and I had no reason to doubt them, more so the school inspector. But somehow this felt wrong.

My Standard 1 (Grade 3) teacher had told us a story about how you should 'roei jou bootjie' (row your boat) and 'glo in jou drome' (believe in your dreams). Ever since, I had held onto that story and believed in my dreams. I was so proud to share my dream with the school inspector and the class. I had even imagined his response would be something like, 'Nou maar toe. Dis mooi.' (There we go. That's beautiful.) That's what my mother would say when she encouraged me to believe in my dreams. Why did the school inspector not want me to do the same?

In the weeks and months that followed, I lost my belief in becoming a famous heart surgeon. I no longer spoke about it and the dream slowly died inside of me. The school inspector had killed it once and for all.

2

Born in a sinkhokkie

The incident with the school inspector had me cursing my father for choosing to live in Bream Way. My life might have been different had he chosen a house in a different street or decided not to move to Nooitgedacht in the first place. The kids might not have laughed at me and the school inspector might not have looked at me the way he did, or made that comment.

Yet my father had been so excited when he came home one evening and told my mother that we were moving to Nooitgedacht.

'Ketie! Ketie!' as he affectionately called her. 'Ôs trek Nooitgedacht toe.' (We're moving to Nooitgedacht.)

His smile was ecstatic, spread all the way across the gap where his four front teeth used to be, and his dark-brown eyes sparkled. The news surprised us all. I was five years old. I jumped up and down, unable to contain my glee, along with my six-year-old brother, Francois, and my ten-year-old sister, Mara.

A local municipal official had told my father of this wonderful place that, once the houses were all built, would be one of the most beautiful coloured townships on the Cape Flats. I was elated, conjuring up a place of beautiful colours. 'Daddy! Daddy!' I cried, pulling at my father's jacket. 'Nooitge ... what? Nooitge ... what?'

After a few repeats, I got it right – Nooitgedacht. That evening, there were joyful celebrations in our little household, and I couldn't wait to move into the beautifully coloured township.

We were living in a tiny, one-bedroom shack in an informal settlement on the outskirts of Elsies River, where my mother had given birth to me on a miserable, wet Saturday morning on 5 August 1967. The

Chinese call it the Year of the Goat or Fire Sheep. They say people born in that year are calm and gentle, and have fewer health problems. I'm not sure about being calm and gentle, but I certainly did not have fewer health problems; growing up in a one-bedroom shack does not make for health and wellbeing.

My father called the shack 'our little sinkhokkie'. It was made of sack, cardboard and rusty corrugated-iron sheets held in place by a few wobbly wooden poles. Its ramshackle fragility set it apart from the other, sturdier shacks; it looked as if the merest sneeze of the south-easter would cause it to collapse. At night, you could hear the wind seething through the gaping holes in the rusty iron sheets. Except for the thin shaft of sunlight that came through the creaky front door or the tiny back window, it was always dark inside, with a foggy haze from the kerosene lamp and candles.

Even though this was my home, there were two things I hated about living in it. Number one was winter. Somehow, our shack was always the first to be flooded. I'm not sure whether this was a case of bad location or sheer bad luck, but by the time the first few millimetres of rain had fallen, our shack was already knee-deep in water. With my father at work, it was left to my mother to salvage whatever she could of our few belongings, but no matter how carefully she prepared for the season, all the holes in the walls and roof meant that our clothes inevitably ended up drenched. Of course, wet clothes meant getting a cold, and on one occasion I was hospitalised with pneumonia, forcing my poor mother to run frantically between a flooded shack and the hospital, afraid that I was about to die.

The other thing I hated about our shack was the outside bucket toilet. If my early childhood trauma has a fixed start, that was it. Not a day went by without my putting up a voracious fight and refusing to use it. As kind and gentle as my mother was, my screams and kicks didn't move her an inch when she dragged me to the toilet. Sitting on that pot felt like eternal damnation. I was convinced that the stench and darkness were colluding to pull me into that filthy, smelly hole, never to appear again. Looking back now, I think of it as my first sense of poverty.

Fed up with my screams and fights, my mother eventually relented and allowed me to use the open space around our shack as my personal toilet. But this brought with it another terror: our neighbour's dog, who always roamed around whenever I was relieving myself. When I squatted, he would charge in my direction and I would run, screaming for my mother, with faeces running down my skinny little legs.

Despite these experiences, I loved our shanty place. When we moved, I would miss running carefree with the other 'kaalgat laaities' (bare-bum children) around the neighbours' shacks, and being cared for as if we shared a whole community of parents. But I was all too happy that we were moving to Nooitgedacht.

3

The curse of Bream Way

We arrived in Nooitgedacht in the middle of the night, in an old Bedford truck that my father had unofficially borrowed from work to transport our few belongings. Even though it was dark, I couldn't wait to see what our new house looked like. As soon as the truck came to a stop, Francois and I jumped off and raced to reach the house first.

Inside was a different world. I was dumbstruck by the size and beauty of the house – three bedrooms with brick walls. A feeling of deep satisfaction overcame me. A short while before, I had been living in a shack, and now here I was, standing in the middle of a proper house. While Mara helped my parents offload the truck, Francois and I ran from one room to another, turning the light switches on and off. I had never had electricity before. Being able to switch on a light felt like learning how to do magic.

For most of the evening, we ran around the house, playing hide-and-seek. Eventually, we ended up at the toilet. Déjà vu. I was frightened and refused to step inside. It took a lot of persuading by Francois before I gave in and entered, but once inside, I was in total awe of the magical flushing toilet. I couldn't get enough of it. We flushed the evening away, trying to figure out where the water came from and where it went.

The next morning I woke up with the same sense of excitement as the night before. What did Nooitgedacht look like during the day? After all, it was supposed to be one of the most beautifully coloured townships on the Cape Flats. Mara, Francois and I couldn't wait to run out of the door, but when we did, the excitement of the previous evening was abruptly and cruelly extinguished.

Outside was a gigantic construction site. Everywhere were half-built homes, cranes and construction vehicles. All around us, workmen were finishing off homes and laying bricks for new ones. Not far from our house, huge cranes were being used to erect four-storey blocks of flats. In our own street, there were already two-storey blocks known as maisonettes. Nothing resembled the colourful images I'd had in mind. All I saw was building dust, chalky sand and this construction site. Completed homes stood on barren land, fenced-off with chicken wire.

As we explored, we came across a pile of logs. It looked as if an entire forest had been cleared to make way for Nooitgedacht. I did not know whether the municipal official had lied to my father or if my little mind was playing a horrible trick on me. Confused, I brushed these thoughts aside as I clung to Mara's hand, hoping that Nooit-gedacht would eventually become the beautiful, coloured township of my imagination.

But, as time went by, I realised that we'd landed up in the poorest part of the area and that we were not alone. The two- and four-storey flats in Bream Way and a few other streets also housed people like us, most of whom had been living in shacks in the same outlying areas of Elsies River. It didn't take long to figure out how so many poor people had landed up here. It all had to do with what my mother and father occasionally spoke of in hushed tones, about people being forced from the homes where they once lived. District Six, Goodwood and Die Akkers were names I often overheard. I didn't make much of it until my parents drove us through Goodwood and told us about forced removals. 'Anne dag was dit ôsse plek,' my father said, his face visibly sad. 'Die wit mense het dit van ôs mense afgevat.' (Once, this was our place. The white people took it from our people.)

'Hoekom, Daddy?' Francois asked. (Why, Daddy?)

'Dis oor apartheid,' he replied. (It's because of apartheid.)

'Wat is apartheid?' I asked. (What is apartheid?)

After a brief lull, my mother quipped, 'Wit mense.' (White people.) I was baffled.

Forced removals had a knock-on effect. My father was lured to move to Nooitgedacht so that the sinkhokkies in Elsies River could be demol-ished to make way for another group of forcefully removed people. The houses, flats, maisonettes and semi-detached homes in Nooitgedacht were intended to cram vast numbers of people next to and on top of one another. Years later, I learnt that apartheid's forced removals were a crude adaptation of Nazi Germany's *Lebensraum* (living spaces) policy. The best land was reserved for the 'superior race' and all other 'inferior races' were removed from it, with many landing up in Nazi ghettos. Nooitgedacht was no different, and in time, most of the Cape Flats was turned into one huge apartheid ghetto. Trapped in these spaces, people sought comfort in whatever trivial advantages they could cling to. I found comfort in the fact that our house and another were the only freestanding homes in Bream Way. They stood on a single plot each, and were a little bigger than the apartments in the maisonettes and semi-detached homes.

Soon, locals dubbed the flats the 'vaal' and 'pink' flats, after their dull grey and off-pink colours. The vaal flats were more scruffy than the pink flats, so people sometimes called them 'die skurwe flats'.

The way we spoke was considered a problem. Many of us on the Cape Flats could have traced our roots to the indigenous Khoikhoi, who'd inhabited the region long before the first Dutch settlers arrived in 1652. Our indigenous forebears spoke Khoekhoe (pronounced Kwêkwê), |Xam, ||Gana and Naro. But history wasn't kind to them; their languages were systematically wiped out and our ancestors, their descendants, ended up speaking Afrikaans and some English. My family spoke Afrikaans and only a little bit of English.

We did not speak these languages the way white people did. I don't know whether our ancestors intentionally decided to make a mess of them or simply created their own home-grown dialect. Either way, we thrashed both languages. Pronouncing the English word 'flats' alongside the Afrikaans word 'skurwe' was but one such example. The flats became 'die flêtse' and so it was that we referred to them as 'die skurwe flêtse' and 'die pienk flêtse'. Even the two-storey maisonettes couldn't escape this dialect, as we crudely reduced this elegant French word to 'die mysonets'.

As more and more people moved into the area, Bream Way began to brim with life. Francois and I were quick to make friends with Errol and Brian, two boys about our age, whose family had moved into one of the maisonettes opposite our house. Uncle Sam Cox, an old friend of my father's, moved into a maisonette with his family not too far down the road. He worked as a plumber in neighbouring Bishop Lavis. We loved Uncle Sam despite his being drunk most of the time. Before going to work, he often stopped at the local smokkie (shebeen) in the vaal flats for his daily dose of cheap Oom Tas or Virginia wine. By the time he went to work, he could hardly mount his bicycle. His wife usually had to pick him up and drag him home. Sometimes, Francois and I did the dragging.

For a while, life in Bream Way seemed normal, like the way it had been in Elsies River. The street was always full of children playing games, from soccer and cricket to on-on, hide-and-seek, kennetjie (a stick game) and bok-bok, my favourite. In bok-bok, two or more kids bent down as the bok-bok, holding tightly onto each other in tandem, with the kid in front holding onto a fixed pole. The other kids, as many as there might be, took turns jumping onto the backs of the bok-bok kids. The one who jumped first had to make sure that he or she landed as close to the pole as possible, so as to leave enough space for the rest. By the time it was my turn (I always made sure I was the last), you could hear the moans and groans of the bok-bok kids struggling underneath the weight of those on top. Being the last meant I had the honour of jumping with as much force as I could muster to collapse the bok-bok. It was great fun with no consideration for the danger of injuries.

Similarly, it never occurred to me that a danger far greater than bok-bok lurked in the shadows. One day, while Francois and I were playing in the street, blissfully unaware of what was happening around us, I heard my mother frantically calling our names.

'Francois! Charles! Kom nou huistoe.' (Come home now.)

From the tone of her voice, I knew something was wrong. We obeyed, my heart pounding as I tried to figure out what it was we may have done but shouldn't have done, or what we didn't do but should have done. At the door, we were hauled into the house, only to discover that we weren't in trouble and that the other children had been called home too. Mara was already inside, and, in an instant, the entire street was empty.

From the window, I saw a group of young men heading in the direction of the vaal flats. Some wore balaclavas or handkerchiefs to hide their faces, and they were armed with bricks, homemade shields and pangas.

Terrified, I hid behind my mother, occasionally peeping out. 'Mommy! Mommy! Who are they?'

'Skollies,' she said.

'What are skollies, Mommy?'

Annoyed, she said, 'They rob and kill people.'

I knew then that what was happening outside was very, very serious.

I recognised two of the young men passing our house. 'Mommy! Mommy!' I shouted. 'Look! There's Boy and Derrick, from around the corner.'

Francois joined in. 'Yes! Yes! There they are.'

'Are they skollies too?'

She gave me a harsh look. I couldn't understand how Boy and Derrick could be skollies; we knew them well. They would stand on the corner, hanging out with their friends, while we played in the street. It had never occurred to me that they might want to rob us, let alone kill us. On the contrary, they were always friendly.

Meanwhile, one of the skollies had moved ahead of the pack to the lamp post where we'd been playing bok-bok a short while before. Hiding behind it, he whistled in the direction of the vaal flats, as if signalling. After a brief lull, he shouted, 'Djy! Djy! Jou ma se poes!' At those words, my mother hurriedly dragged us to our bedroom. Mara followed suit to her room.

The memory of what followed remains vivid. From our bedroom, we could hear the chorus of young men shouting, 'Djy! Djy! Jou ma se poes! Staan vas, jou naai! Jou ma se poes!' I had no idea what they were shouting, but it sounded rhythmic.

It wasn't long before I heard bricks thudding onto the street, presumably thrown in the direction of Bream Way. Next came the screech of pangas scraped across the concrete road, followed by more shouts: 'Djy! Djy! Jou ma se poes! Staan vas, jou naai!'

'What are they doing?' I asked Francois, terrified. 'What are they doing?'

'They're fighting the other skollies in the vaal flats,' he said.

After a while I asked, 'What does "Djy! Jou ma se poes" mean?'

He stared at me without saying a word and then resumed listening to what was happening outside.

With bricks falling, pangas scraping and petrol bombs exploding, you could follow the fighting as the two gangs chased each other up and down the street. From the sound of it, the gang from the vaal flats had made inroads into Bream Way. And so it went on until a gunshot changed everything. A silence fell for a short while before a voice yelled, 'Ôs het hom! Ôs het hom! Kappie naai vrek!' (We've got him! We've got him! Chop the fucker dead!)

They'd shot someone. I started to cry. Meanwhile my mother was spurred into prayer as she checked that all the doors and windows were locked: 'Here! Beskerm tog hierdie huis. Ek bestraf die duiwel se magte hier buite.' (God! Please protect this house. I rebuke the devil's powers outside.)

After a while, we heard police sirens in the distance. I immediately stopped crying and my mother stopped praying. Francois and I rushed outside, curious to see what had happened.

Slowly, people emerged from their homes. The street looked like a warzone. Bricks lay scattered all over, as did the charred remains of broken bottles used for petrol bombs. The gangsters from both sides had disappeared, except for a lone young man lying face down in the middle of the street, close to the vaal flats. A police vehicle pulled up next to him. My body trembled as I followed Francois and Mara to the scene, ignoring my mother's protests. A lot of people had already congregated.

As I got closer, I peeped through the crowd. The wounded boy lay in a pool of blood. He was young, just a few years older than Mara. Not long afterwards, a woman ran towards the scene from the vaal flats, crying hysterically. The boy's mother, I guessed. The police stopped her from touching her son as they waited for the ambulance to arrive. I couldn't understand why they held her back. Maybe, I thought, it's because of all the blood around him.

Emotions soon ran high. A plump woman from the flats wearing a kopdoekie (headscarf) accused a Bream Way woman of having a gang-ster for a son.

'Ja! Jou kind is 'n fokken skollie!' she shouted. (Yes! Your child is a fucking gangster!)

Others chimed in and a war of words erupted. The police quickly intervened and pushed each side apart. Eventually the ambulance arrived. The paramedics performed first aid, then placed the wounded boy on a stretcher and took him to the hospital.

That evening, I could hardly sleep. Francois and I shared a double bed and I held tightly onto him. Images of the skollies, Boy, Derrick and the bloody young man flashed through my mind, along with the sound of scraping pangas. And those strange words: 'Djy! Djy! Jou ma se poes!'

A few days later, I learnt that the boy had survived and been dis-charged from hospital. I never got to know his real name, but some knew him as 'Piele' (Penises). Piele had apparently left school after barely making it to Standard 4, and started breaking into homes and stealing from the local shop. Some pitied him, saying he was only trying to make a living. From there, it was merely a matter of time before he joined the gang in the vaal flats.

Relative calm returned to Bream Way soon enough. Kids played in the street. Boy, Derrick and their friends loitered at their usual spot on the street corner. I decided not to venture near them. The Bream Way gang they belonged to was named the Terrible Josters, or simply the Josters, and the gang from the vaal flats was the Flat Boys. The fight I'd witnessed was part of a turf war. Bream Way belonged to the Josters, while the vaal flats were the territory of the Flat Boys. No one dared cross into the other's territory. Though we lived in Bream Way, our house served as the imaginary marker separating the two territories. You could say we were at the epicentre of the gang war in Nooitgedacht, able to observe each and every fight as if we were part of it all.

One day, Francois and I decided to imitate a gang fight. I played the role of a Joster and he was a Flat Boy. As we fought with our sticks, chasing each other up and down our backyard, the excitement got the better of me. Without thinking, I yelled, 'Djy! Djy! Jou ma se poes!'

I knew something terrible was coming my way when I saw my mother charging in my direction. The next moment, I was given a moerse harde klap (one hell of a hard smack) that knocked me to the ground.

'Laat ek nog net een keer hoor jy sê daai woorde, dan sal jy sien wat ek met jou maak. Ek trek jou gatvelle van jou af!' (Let me hear you saying those words just one more time, and you'll see what I'll do to you. I'll tear the skin off your arse!) Then she turned and furiously walked away. It was the first time I'd experienced her wrath.

Francois comforted me while I wiped my tears, and finally explained what those words meant, giggling with embarrassment as he pointed to his private parts. 'Mans het piepies en vroue, toeties,' he said. (Men have penises and women, vaginas.) 'The gangsters swear at the toetie between a woman's legs.'

We giggled, but it puzzled me that they swore at a woman's toetie and not at a man's piepie. It took me a while to figure out that 'jou ma se poes' was not only the crudest, most derogatory of insults, but also a curse on a mother for having given birth to the targeted person. No wonder my mother had not wanted us to hear those words. She had good reason to be furious when I'd used them.

Over the months and years, the fighting between the two gangs became more frequent and intense. Certain self-imposed rules developed among the residents. By 8 p.m., there wasn't a soul to be seen in Bream Way and almost all of the lights were switched off. In their homes, however, people jockeyed for the best positions behind their drawn curtains, as if waiting for their open-air entertainment. The gangsters on each side would then emerge, ready to fight. My mother pleaded for us to go to bed, but we didn't want to miss the action outside either. Against her wishes, we'd tiptoe into the lounge to peep though the curtains.

By this time though, my mother was more worried about my father's safety than about us sneaking around behind her back. In addition to working as a truck driver for the *Cape Argus* newspaper, my father was also a lay preacher at a 'handeklapkerkie' (handclapping church). Our handeklapkerkie, like most others operating on the Cape Flats, gathered informally at the homes of its congregants. Unlike mainstream churches, they believed in 'die wedergeboorte' (being born again), speaking in tongues, and baptism by accepting Jesus Christ as your personal Lord and Saviour. They operated on the scriptural injunction in Matthew 18:20: 'For where two or three gather in my name, there I am with them.'

Handeklapkerkies were often ridiculed for being disorderly so I dreaded the embarrassment of going to church, but Sundays were always worth it for the chance to see Sister Babs. She was the mother of all mothers when it came to speaking in tongues. No sooner had the congregation started singing a moving Pinksterkoortjie (Pentecostal hymn) than she'd be on her feet, presumably spurred on by the Holy Spirit. With her hands held high, she'd ululate strange words – 'Halala jebosho kalabash! Halala jebosho kalabash!' Soon, others would join in while the rest remained deep in prayer. No one was supposed to watch, as church elders deemed it too sacred to be seen by the naked eye, but I peeped. Sister Babs was hilarious.

My father attended church most nights and speaking in tongues was a long, drawn-out affair, so he always arrived home late at night. One evening, after a particularly vicious street fight, with gun-toting gangsters running up and down, firing indiscriminately at each other, my mother was at her wits' end. It was a mini-war outside, with the sound of automatic gunfire. We had taken shelter in our bedrooms. My mother prayed, and cursed my father.

A few minutes after the gang fight ceased, his old Volkswagen kombi came rattling to a stop in front of our house. From the way my mother opened the door, I could sense she was livid.

'Hoekom is jy altyd so blerrie laat? Jy stel jou lewe onnodig in gevaar.' (Why are you always so bloody late? You're placing your life in danger unnecessarily.)

He dismissed her concern. 'Hoekom worry djy? Djy wiet wa ek is. Niks sal met my gebeur nie. Die Here is met my.' (Why do you worry? You know where I am. Nothing will happen to me. God is with me.)

He hadn't been home long when there was a knock on the door. My mother peeped through the window before opening up.

'Is Broer Baard hie?' asked an exhausted young man. 'Ôs need transport na Tygerberg Hospitaal.' (Is Brother Baard here? We need transport to Tygerberg Hospital).

My father's name was Frans, but everyone knew him as Broer Baard. His blind mother had called him 'Baard' (Beard) for no apparent reason. 'Broer' (brother) just came with the territory of belonging to a handeklapkerkie.

One of the Josters had been badly stabbed by the Flat Boys, and my father agreed to take him to the hospital. Despite the territorial gang war, my father was the go-to person for both gangs in case of hospital emergencies. This afforded our family a measure of protection from both sides.

'Francois! Charles!' my father shouted. 'Staan op! Kô' saam!' (Get up! Come with!)

I felt a thrill of fear and excitement at the sound of my father's words. He was offering us an opportunity to see who got injured and how badly, so Francois and I wasted no time getting out of bed and running off, despite my mother's fierce objection.

We drove down Bream Way and stopped at Ouma Ross's maisonette. In the dark, two men emerged from the flat, carrying someone by the arms and legs. I reckoned it was Tawali, Ouma Ross's son. He was one of the boys who hung around with Boy and Derrick on the street corner. The two men got into the kombi with him. His clothes and face were covered in blood. His head had been sliced open with a panga and he was hardly moving. I stared at his bloody wound, then swiftly turned away. The gore made me feel uncomfortable. I shifted closer to Francois. Tawali didn't say a word, but moaned occasionally as the pain wracked him. He must have fallen and then been attacked by the Flat Boys. I was surprised they hadn't shot him too.

One of the Josters, known as Station, took off his jersey and put it around Tawali's head to stop the bleeding. There was little conversation as we drove past the vaal flats to Tygerberg Hospital, except that my father wasted no time in trying to convert them.

'Wanne gaan julle manne stop met die dinge en julle harte anie Here gie?' (When are you guys going to stop with these things and give your hearts to God?)

The response was muted. 'Ja, Broer Baard, ôs verstaan.' (Yes, Broer Baard, we understand.)

At the hospital, we drove straight to the emergency entrance. Station got a wheelchair while the other Joster helped Tawali out of the kombi.

'Dankie, Broer Baard,' they called out as we left. (Thanks, Broer Baard.)

In time, I regularly took these trips with my father to Tygerberg Hospital, witnessing first-hand the bloody business of gangsterism. I came to the understanding that Bream Way and the flats were dreadful neighbourhoods. What little sense of community and belonging had existed eventually disappeared and was replaced by something ominous and frightening. Fear and terror were everywhere, and fewer kids played games in the street. Francois and I were confined to our backyard. It felt as if the voices of the children in Bream Way and the flats had fallen silent.

Soon, kids on both sides of the divide began to taunt one another, first at school and then in the streets. James, one of the older boys from the vaal flats, prowled the school playground for kids from Bream Way to bully. For my own protection, I made sure that I played as close to Francois as possible.

Even the short walk through the vaal flats to school became a run-for-your-life nightmare. Kids from the flats would pelt us with stones, shouting, 'Julle Josters!' (You Josters!) This eventually forced us to take a longer walk through Nooitgedacht to get to the school's back gate.

As the situation deteriorated, kids began to stage their own mock gang fights after school. Errol and Brian, our friends from across the street, joined in the fray. With sharpened wooden staves in one hand and stones in the other, children from Bream Way and the vaal flats charged at each other, shouting, 'Up, up! Up, up! Jou ma se poes!'

Some mothers considered it fun, actively encouraging the fighting. Francois and I, however, got a stern warning from our mother: 'As ek julle ná aan daardie kinders vang, dan weet julle wat sal gebeur.' (If I catch you anywhere near those kids, you know what will happen.)

Eventually, these mock fights acted as curtain-raisers to the real gang fights in the evenings. Word soon spread, and some schoolteachers started to refer to those from Bream Way and the flats as 'little skollies'. No matter how hard I tried to distance myself, all of us were lumped together. 'Julle bliksems. Julle is mos klein skollies!' they yelled at us. (You devils. You are little gangsters!)

—ᴍ—

Whenever I think back to that day when the school inspector told me not to aim too high, I wonder whether this image of a little skollie was what he had in mind. The hurt he caused me still resonates. Many years later, I saw that hurt poignantly articulated in the movie *Scent of a Woman*, when the blind Lieutenant Colonel Frank Slade, played by Al Pacino, defends Charlie, a college student, before a school assembly. The principal wants Charlie to name three other students who'd engaged in a prank; if he does not, he will face expulsion. In a highly charged retort to the principal, Slade fumes:

> There was a time I could see. And I have seen. Boys like these, younger than these. Their arms torn out, their legs ripped off. But there is nothing like the sight of an amputated spirit. There's no prosthetic for that. You think you're merely sending this splendid foot sol-dier back home … with his tail between his legs, but I say you are executing his SOUL!

That's how I felt that morning after the inspector's criticism – my spirit amputated and my soul executed. It was a dreadful feeling for which I could find no prosthetic.

Yet, there was a part of me that refused to let go and clung to what-ever spirit I had left. I don't know if the daily drudge of Bream Way and the flats planted in me the seeds for my own survival, but it certainly awoke something deep within me, and I held onto it, whatever it was.

4

The tale of two Nooitgedachts

It didn't take long for me to realise that there were two Nooitgedachts
– the one poor and the other somewhat better off. A short walk down
Barracuda Crescent, into Pike Crescent and along Tuna Avenue revealed
a world different to that of Bream Way and the flats. Houses that once
stood on barren, sandy soil were quickly transformed into colourfully
painted and decorated homes with lush green lawns and beautiful gardens – the Nooitgedacht I'd once imagined.

The Dyers of Barracuda Crescent distinguished themselves as the
socialites of Nooitgedacht, while the Adriaans of Pike Crescent were
hard-nosed businesspeople whose charming house had a thatched roof.
In Chad Way stood the picturesque semi-detached house of the elderly
Alexanders. They had the loveliest garden in Nooitgedacht, a dazzling
display of dahlias and an intoxicating, aromatic rose garden. This earned
them the nicknames Ouma and Oupa Blomme (Grandma and Grandpa
Flowers).

Then there was Tuna Avenue, where Peter Marais lived. He was the
most well-known political personality in Nooitgedacht, with a pen-
chant for Elvis Presley impersonations. He went on to become one
of the most colourful politicians on the Cape Flats and eventually the
premier of the Western Cape, until he resigned following allegations
of sexual harassment.

While our house was located at the epicentre of the gang warfare
in Bream Way, Marais's was at the epicentre of what the locals in that
part of Nooitgedacht called 'Little Bishopscourt', in emulation of one of
the most exclusive and expensive white suburbs in Cape Town. People
in Little Bishopscourt not only set themselves apart from the rest of us

with their beautiful homes and gardens, but also acted differently, dressed better, looked healthier and, most of all, exuded confidence and self-assurance. As I grew older, I discovered there was something sinister about this confidence and self-assurance, and it all had to do with the term 'coloured'.

What I had thought of as coloured had nothing to do with colourful images of Nooitgedacht and everything to do with us – *we* were the colours, the *coloureds*, and what categorised us as such was our kroeshare (kinky hair), dik lippe (thick lips), breë neusgate (broad nostrils) and dark-brown skin.

These attributes were considered so despicable that, to some coloured people, they were a curse from which they sought to escape into a fantasy world of white emulation. Those in Little Bishopscourt set the standard with their straight hair, green eyes, narrow noses and lips, and fair skin. The more of these attributes you possessed, the whiter you were. Those who didn't possess them aspired to them. We dubbed them 'die wit mense van Nooitgedacht' (the white people of Nooitgedacht).

The rest of us had to be content with our kroeshare, dik lippe, breë neusgate and, most of all, darker skins. The more you were endowed with these characteristics, the closer you were to the coloured bottom, which was where my family ended up. We were the 'dalits', the 'untouchable' coloureds. So proud were people of staying in Little Bishopscourt that whenever one of us untouchables strayed into their world, we were treated with contempt. I remember visiting a school friend whose mother was so enraged at the sight of me that she wouldn't allow me into their house. I was deemed too dirty to enter. Such occurrences became the norm.

So pervasive was this sense of whiteness that it found its way into my school. Some teachers tended to separate the 'white' kids from the rest of us and this played itself out in a bizarre morning ritual. Before lessons, some teachers stalked around the class with long, supple canes, sniffing out those they called the 'stinkers' and the 'gravediggers'. These were terms given to those of us who smelt unwashed, didn't brush their teeth or whose nails were long and dirty. No matter how hard I tried, I always fell afoul of one of these cardinal sins.

Once you were found to be a stinker or a gravedigger, you were made to stretch out your hands with your palms down to be caned repeatedly over the knuckles. Very rarely were 'white' kids caned; that punishment was reserved for the rest of us. No matter how cruel and perverted this ritual, the teachers always seemed to have some religious justification for their actions. Whenever we were hit over the knuckles, we had to recite, 'Cleanliness is next to godliness. Cleanliness is next to godliness.' I don't know how many times I recited these words while tears streamed down my face. No matter how hard I prayed every night – 'Gentle Jesus, meek and mild, look upon a little child; pity my simplicity, suffer me to come to Thee' – I was inevitably a stinker or a gravedigger.

So I began to wrestle with God: *Why is God so unfair? He forever seems to favour those who are 'white' and clean. What about the rest of us?*

5

My father's heart of darkness

One day after school, Francois and I decided to plant a beautiful garden in front of our house. Perhaps with a garden, we could be a bit more like the white coloureds and stand out from the rest of Bream Way. My mother bought some grass sprigs, carnations and a few small roses, but the soil was barren and required a lot of tilling. I was seven, and the spade was almost as big as me, so I could hardly turn the soil. It was a clumsy affair from the start. I managed to create a few rows before I stumbled upon something I'd wondered about before – the source of the water for the flushing toilet.

I plunged the spade into the ground and water burst forth from the pipe supplying our house. Shocked, I dropped the spade and ran inside as fast as I could.

'Mommy! Mommy!' Francois shouted. 'Come quick!'

In a matter of seconds she and Mara were there, and all hell broke loose. 'Here Jesus!' my mother cried. 'Wat het jy gemaak?' (Lord Jesus! What have you done?)

'It wasn't me, Mommy! It was Charles!' Francois quickly retorted.

By then I was already hiding deep underneath the bed, my heart pounding. I knew I'd done something terrible, but I wasn't sure exactly how terrible it was.

In the distance, I heard my mother shouting at Francois: 'Here Jesus! Doen iets! Stop die water!' (Lord Jesus! Do something! Stop the water!)

I could hear Mara and Francois's frantic efforts. After a considerable commotion, things went completely quiet. Eventually, Francois came into the room, looking for me.

'Where are you? I know you're in here. You can come out now, it's all okay,' he said. I slowly emerged from underneath the bed. 'An uncle from up the street came to switch off the main water supply, but now we don't have water. The pipe still needs to be fixed.'

'What will Daddy say?' I asked anxiously, looking for reassurance.

He shrugged. 'I don't know.'

I began to cry, unsure of what was in store for me. I didn't leave the room for the rest of the day.

When my father returned home that evening, I was in bed and pulled the blanket over my head, pretending to be fast asleep. I heard my mother open the front door before heading to the kitchen to prepare his food. It was routine for her to keep his supper warm no matter what time he got home. That's how he wanted it.

I was anxious to hear their conversation. After some initial mumbling, I heard my mother say, 'I must tell you something.' She paused and then continued. 'While I was working in the garden, I accidently damaged the underground water pipe and now we're without water. It was an accident and I'm really sorry.'

I was surprised that she'd taken the blame, but realised she was protecting me from a hiding. I sighed with relief; I was in the clear, nothing to worry about.

Everything went quiet. I was so happy that I began to emerge from under the blanket, when a huge bang reverberated throughout the house. It sounded like fireworks, but it was my father's fist pounding the kitchen table. 'Ek wêk my fokken gat af en djy sien kans ommie blêrrie hys af te briek!' he yelled. (I work my fucking arse off and you see fit to break down the bloody house!)

Terrified, I darted back under the blanket and held tightly onto Francois. My father had never spoken to my mother like that. He was always kind and polite.

The next moment I heard my mother's frantic cries: 'Frans! Frans! Moet my nie slaan nie!' (Frans! Frans! Don't hit me!)

This was followed by a desperate scuffle, glasses breaking and someone falling to the ground. My mother was screaming, begging for her life.

'Frans! Frans! Moet my nie doodmaak nie!' (Frans! Frans! Don't kill me!)

I started crying. 'Francois! Francois! Why is Daddy hitting Mommy?' I clung to him.

'Don't cry! Don't cry!' he told me in a teary, quivering voice as he held me.

Next, I heard footsteps. My mother must have tried to get away, as her voice now came from the passage. From the punches and smacks and what sounded like her head being bashed against the wall, I could tell my father had caught her again. She squealed as he gave her one blow after the other.

A further scuffle ensued and then the front door was opened and banged closed as my mother fled the house, my father in pursuit. A sudden quiet returned. By then, I was soaked in tears. I couldn't believe this was my father, the person I loved so dearly.

Sometime later, he returned and finished eating in the kitchen. I cried myself to sleep.

I don't know what happened to my mother that night, but in the morning I was woken by a ghastly squealing. It was as if the horror had never ended.

'Can't it stop? Can't it stop?' I cried to Francois.

My mother must have snuck back into the house in the middle of the night, and spent the evening sleeping in the lounge, where my father found her. Not satisfied with his savagery from the previous evening, he carried on. The anguish I heard coming from deep inside my mother that morning haunted me for years. It was the kind of cry Joseph Conrad describes in *Heart of Darkness*: 'a cry, a very loud cry, as of infinite desolation, soared slowly in the opaque air … A complaining clamour … as though the mist itself had screamed.' That morning, it sounded as if my father had opened the gates of hell.

Only after he'd satisfied his cruelty did he leave for work, and only then did Mara, Francois and I get out of bed and slowly make our way to the lounge. Our house resembled the warzone I'd so often seen outside after a gang fight: broken glass and overturned chairs with blood spattered against the passage wall. I expected the worst.

In the lounge, my mother was slumped on the couch, her face bruised and battered. Blood oozed from her mouth. Her eyes were swollen. I hardly recognised her. Mara and Francois just stared at her, not saying a word. I began to cry.

'Mommy! Mommy! Where's my Mommy?' I cried, clinging to Francois's hand.

'Come! Come! Come to me,' she mumbled, beckoning.

I was too afraid, and cried harder. 'No! No! I don't want to!'

I'd never seen my mother like this. Mara had tears rolling down behind her tiny glasses. Francois stood there, eyes dry. He didn't say a word. The night before I had sensed what hatred was, but that morning I saw it on my brother's face. It was as if his heart had turned cold and whatever tears he may have had were frozen by the hatred he felt towards my father. In her mumblings, my mother told Mara to get us ready for school. Then she slumped back into the couch. Turning her head into the cushions, she went on crying with a kind of infinite sorrow.

That morning, the happy family of my childhood was shattered. My father, the hero figure, was gone. My mother, reduced to a pulp, landed up in hospital, where she stayed for a week.

The sombre mood that had befallen Bream Way settled on our house. Life was different now.

6

Give me this day my daily bread

After my mother was discharged from hospital, relative calm returned to our house. There was a semblance of normality and even my father seemed his usual self. He came home earlier and we went out as a family more often, in the battered red and white combi. The old rattily-tatty engine made more noise than an engine should, and most of the time it had to be jump-started with a push. My father explained that this was because the brushes of the starter motor were worn.

But if it wasn't the brushes, then it was the carburettor that flooded with petrol. No matter how often my father took the kombi to his backyard mechanic, it always came back worse than before. So bad, in fact, that we joked that the mechanic was fixing it broken. None of this stopped us from driving old rattily-tatty to the beach or to see the New Year's lights or the Kaapse Klopse (Cape Minstrels). The combi even took us on family trips to Ceres, about two hundred kilometres from Cape Town, where we saw my father in action. It was his life's mission to preach among the poor, destitute and mostly drunk farmworkers. This is where I saw the father I loved, different from the one who abused my mother – a father who was kind, gentle and compassionate, treating strangers as if they were his own kin.

It baffled me that someone so deeply religious who had devoted his life to others could perpetrate cruelty towards his own wife. As I grew older, I wondered whether it had to do with the way in which he interpreted Bible scriptures like Colossians 3:18: 'Wives, submit yourselves unto your husbands, as it is fit in the Lord.' Whether true or not, my father certainly gave literal expression to Genesis 9:7: 'And you, be ye fruitful, and multiply; bring forth abundantly in the earth, and multiply therein.'

By the time I was twelve years old, my siblings included Roseline, Christopher, Marius, Amanda, Ronel and Anneline. After a short break, Johan and Lorenzo were born in quick succession. My mother gave birth to eleven of us in total. Had it not been for a few miscarriages, we would have been an even larger family.

Having old rattily-tatty came in handy, but our three-bedroom house became too small. My mother and father slept in the big room, Mara and Roseline in the small room. The rest of us were squeezed into the middle room. Amanda, Ronel and Anneline shared a double-bunk in one corner; Johan and, later, Lorenzo, got a cot in the other corner. Christopher and Marius had to share the double bed with Francois and me. We slept head to feet, like sardines.

The speed at which our family increased far outpaced any increases in my father's meagre truck-driver's salary. He received his wages every Thursday, and by the time the bills were paid – the home instalment, the doodgenootskap (burial society policy), the clothing lay-by, the Christmas hamper and the furniture accounts – there was hardly any money left for food. Nevertheless, Friday, Saturday and Sunday were good days in our household, and we could even share some food with friends and visitors. On Monday and Tuesday, the lean time set in. Wednesday was touch and go, and by Thursday there was nothing left to eat.

Monday at least provided a bit of a bonus. My father religiously brought home a plastic bag full of leftovers from his boss's Sunday lunch. He called it 'skrepkos' (scrap food), and it was meant for our dog, Sheba. It was always red because the beetroot mixed with the rice, discarded potatoes, and half-eaten meat and chicken pieces. This was a meal on its own, and us kids had no intention of allowing Sheba to enjoy it all by herself. We'd finish most of it before a few bare bones got anywhere near her plate.

Thursday was a day of fasting with not a morsel in sight until my father returned home in the evening. Kids at school taunted me as a loafer and avoided me on Thursdays; they knew it was my begging day.

One Thursday, when I was unsuccessful with my begging, I turned to the school's dirt bins. Pretending to throw rubbish away, I secretly scavenged for any discarded bread. I found none, and knew it was going to be a long, hungry day.

When I got home that afternoon, I went straight to the kitchen to see if there was anything to eat. There was nothing. I drank some water in the hope that it would ease my hunger pangs, and went outside to sit in the sun. I found a corner next to our house and sat down, head between my legs.

Sheba roused herself and walked sluggishly towards me. I could count her ribs, she was that thin. Her eyes were droopy, and from the way she walked, I knew she hadn't eaten in days. She licked my face and I pushed her away.

'No, Sheba. Go away! Go away!'

She kept on licking and eventually I gave up. After a while, our neighbour's back door opened. A big, imposing figure emerged: Mrs Sasman, wife of the schoolteacher Mr Sasman. They had three children, about the same ages as Mara, Francois and me.

She carried a plate of bread.

'Charles,' she said, 'here's some old bread for Sheba. Please give it to her.'

'Thank you, Mrs Sasman,' I said politely. The bread was stale, some of it flecked with greyish mould. Sheba had heard her name and was jumping at me, forcing me to throw the bread on the ground for her to eat. I handed the plate back to Mrs Sasman.

When she closed the door, I dived to the ground, scrabbling with Sheba for my share. She growled at me, having already swallowed most of the scraps. I managed to snatch a few pieces from her mouth before she ran off with the rest. I wiped the sand off and ate. After this meagre meal, I went inside to sleep. By the time my father got home that evening, I was still asleep, and missed out on the food he brought home.

I was not the only one begging for bread; there were many other kids in my situation. One in particular stood out: Benjamin, a tiny boy from Bishop Lavis. Almost every morning, before the school bell rang, he'd stand at the school gate, begging for bread: 'Stukkie diat, asseblief.' (Piece of bread, please.) In time, this earned him the unenviable nickname of 'Stukkie Diat'.

One morning, it so happened that my mother had wrapped four of the most delicious slices of soft white bread packed with cheese and tomatoes for my lunch. This was an unusual treat, and I was looking forward to showing off my bread at school. Usually, I only had dry brown bread, with the occasional smear of peanut butter and jam, wrapped in flimsy Cartwright wrapping paper. As I approached the gate, I saw Stukkie Diat and became anxious. I hid my bread behind my back, but it was too late; he'd seen it.

'Charles, my broe, stukkie diat, asseblief,' he begged. (Charles, my brother, piece of bread, please.)

I acted as if I hadn't heard or seen him and briskly walked on. But he caught up with me.

'Asseblief, my broe.' (Please, my brother.)

I tried to ignore him, but his little brown eyes stared at me. *Djirre, Stukkie Diat. Hoekom vandag van alle dae?* I cursed (*Jees, Stukkie Diat. Why today of all days?*), but I could see he was hungry. I wavered for a moment. My head said no; my heart said yes. Something inside prompted me to hand my entire sandwich parcel to him. Later that day, I regretted my actions. Not only did I go hungry, but I never got to show off my most delicious sandwiches to my classmates either.

7

Will the misery ever end?

Life in Bream Way could best be described as a seesaw – up one moment and down the next. Most often it was down. The gang fights got worse, the stabbings and killings happened more frequently, and the semblance of peace at home routinely broke down. Although my father restrained himself from further assaulting my mother, they frequently quarrelled. I found myself in a merciless spiral with no end in sight.

Yet just a few streets away, life seemed perfectly normal, with happy families of mothers, fathers and children. I often wished I'd been born into one of those happy families instead of the hell of my daily life. But we weren't the only ones caught up in this spiral.

Late one evening, when I was about fifteen, there was a frantic knocking on our front door. It was Aunty Dora from down the road.

'Is jou pa hie? Sê hy moet gou kô'!' she sobbed. 'Ek het vi' Jan mettie mes gestiek!' (Is your father here? Tell him to come quickly! I stabbed Jan with the knife!)

My father was at church and my mother was working the nightshift as an assistant nurse at an old-age home. Mara, who was looking after the younger kids, immediately summoned Francois and me to help Aunty Dora while she called the police and an ambulance.

We followed Aunty Dora to her maisonette, where we found Uncle Jan lying face down on the bed. We knew him as a gentle, soft-spoken man who wouldn't kill a fly when sober, but when drunk, he would turn violent and chase Aunty Dora up and down the street with a kitchen knife, threatening to kill her. Aunty Dora was a gracious woman, forever immaculately dressed. When she walked past our house to church, her eyes were often badly bruised and swollen, but she hid them behind her sunglasses. Even then, she maintained good posture, keeping her head up and greeting politely.

Now, she waited in the next bedroom with her two small children while we attended to Uncle Jan. I could smell the alcohol oozing from his body, but there was no blood on his clothes. We turned him over to look for the stab wound and, after taking off his shirt, noticed a small incision underneath his left breast.

'Uncle Jan! Uncle Jan! Wake up!' I shouted frantically.

His eyes were closed and he was breathing heavily.

'Uncle Jan! Uncle Jan!' Francois pleaded. 'Talk to us. Please talk to us.'

A tearful Aunty Dora came into the room. 'Is he okay? Will he be okay?'

'Don't worry, Aunty Dora,' said Francois, 'go to your room.' Then he told me to run home and ask Mara to urgently phone again for the police and an ambulance.

I did so and then raced back to help Francois. He looked at me and, with a tremor in his voice, said, 'Hy ganitie makie.' (He's not going to make it.)

Uncle Jan growled as he gasped for air.

'What are we going to do?' I shouted at Francois, panicking.

'I don't know! There's nothing we can do.'

The growling became fainter. Francois and I had learnt a little bit of first aid, so we performed mouth-to-mouth resuscitation, hoping it would help with his airflow. It was all in vain. His growling stopped and Uncle Jan no longer gasped for air. By then Aunty Dora was in the room, having rushed in after hearing my shouts.

'Is hy dood? Is hy dood?' (Is he dead? Is he dead?)

We looked at her, unsure how to respond. Eventually Francois said, 'Dit lyk so, Aunty Dora.' (It looks like it, Aunty Dora.)

She broke down and cried uncontrollably.

We stood there, not knowing what to do, but we'd grown accustomed to comforting our mother when she'd suffered our father's verbal and emotional abuse, so we took turns hugging her. It was more than two hours before the police and ambulance arrived. While the paramedics were busy with Uncle Jan's body, Aunty Dora told the police how she'd fended off her husband's knife attack and stabbed him in the heart in defence.

'I didn't mean to kill him,' she sobbed.

The police had taken a long time to arrive, but a female officer tried to comfort Aunty Dora. It was one of the rare instances when I saw the police show sympathy. Many months later, we were relieved to learn that Aunty Dora would not face any charges for the death of Uncle Jan.

But not every tragic incident had a happy ending: witness the case of Henna and Billy, Bream Way's own socialite couple. Billy was strong and athletic, and Henna bubbly and full of energy. They'd often walk past our house to the vaal flats, hand in hand and smiling happily.

'Hello, Aunty Ketie,' Henna would greet my mother. 'Die kinners raak nou mooi groot.' (The children are growing nice and big.)

'Julle twee moet mooi na julleself kyk,' Billy would chime in. (You two must look after yourselves.)

But later in the afternoon, they were a different couple. Stone drunk, they would stagger home, swearing profusely at each other, yet helping each other along the way.

One afternoon, things got particularly heated as they progressed along Bream Way.

'Is lankal dat djy agter my fokken rug naai,' Henna yelled at Billy, accusing him of having an affair behind her back.

'Moenie met my fokken kak praat nie,' Billy shouted back. (Don't talk fucking shit to me.) He picked up a brick, walked over to where Henna stood and smacked her in the face with it.

I watched in disbelief as Henna tumbled to the ground. The next moment, people rushed to where she lay motionless, blood oozing from her head. Billy had disappeared.

'Call the ambulance! Call the police!' people shouted. Henna vomited into a pool of her own blood.

By the time the police and ambulance arrived, the people of Bream Way were up in arms, baying for Billy's blood. 'Die naai! Hy sal sien wat ôs met hom sal maak. Die ma se poes.' (The fuck! He'll see what we'll do to him. The motherfucker.) Henna was rushed to hospital.

When she was discharged, months later, she wasn't the same, and she'd been paralysed from the waist down. Billy had been arrested and was found guilty of assault, but he served only six months in jail. Despite her ordeal, Henna's spirit was indomitable. She still greeted us warmly as she rolled her wheelchair past our house. Billy was never seen again.

If we'd all had Henna's spirit, Bream Way might have been a good place to live. But it never was; instead, we turned on one another, again and again. Take our next-door neighbour Mr Sasman, for example.

He had never felt at home in Nooitgedacht, and dreaded every moment. He frequently quibbled with Tokman, who lived in a maisonette opposite him. Some said Tokman was a drug merchant, as shadowy characters always frequented his flat late at night, allegedly conducting shady deals behind closed doors. Many people liked him nevertheless.

Sasman, however, couldn't stand the sight of Tokman at his maisonette window, calmly smoking a slow-boat (joint) while he gazed at those below. This was an invitation for cruel rebuke.

'Jou fokken merchant gemors. Dis wat djy is,' Sasman would yell at him. (You fucking merchant rubbish. That's what you are.)

Tokman's retort was even more damning. 'Hey! Djy's 'n fokken meit, djy. Kô' yt, jou naai! Ek sal jou fokken vrekmaak, jou tief.' (Hey! You're a fucking bitch. Come out you fuck! I'll fucking kill you, you bitch.)

And so it carried on, sometimes for days, followed by long lulls as if they were the most peaceful of neighbours.

One Saturday morning, Sasman took his frustration with our neighbourhood out on us. Francois had been keeping chicks in our backyard and woke up to find that they had escaped from their cage and were roaming freely in Sasman's garden. 'Shu! Shu!' he called, frantically trying to woo them back as he leaned over the fence, still in his short pyjama pants. Leaning next to him, I 'shu-shued' too. We feared something bad might happen if Sasman saw the chicks, as he often cut up soccer balls that landed in his garden. But it was too late. Sasman emerged from his house with a spade. When Francois saw it, he started to cry and pleaded with Sasman not to hurt his chicks. I ran into the house yelling, 'Mommy! Mommy!'

When my mother and I got outside, Sasman was calmly bludgeoning the chicks to death one by one. My mother flew into a rage, yelling at Sasman. 'Stop! Jou blerrie monster! Stop!' (Stop! You bloody monster! Stop!)

Sasman didn't care, and continued. Then he picked up the ones that were still alive and broke their necks. When he was done, he threw the dead chicks over the fence into our yard.

'Jou vark!' my mother scolded Sasman. 'Het jy geen ontsag vir die kleintjies nie?' (You pig! Don't you have any compassion for little kids?) Francois cried like a baby as he cradled the dead chicks in his arms.

Unruffled, Sasman spat at my mother while his wife and children looked on, waving his spade at her and daring her to cross into his yard. His hatred was so intense that he yelled, 'Jy maak mos jou kinders groot vir die galg.' (You're rearing your children for the gallows.)

I don't know what caused Sasman to utter those words. It hurt a lot. However, this didn't stop us from playing with his children and respecting his wife, who never seemed to approve of his actions, even though she quietly remained by his side.

But not all of life in Bream Way was about cruelty, bloodshed and death. There remained pockets where life provided a measure of joy and happiness. When there were no gang fights, we played with exuberance, and the sound of our laughter reverberated while Bob Marley's 'No Woman, No Cry' and Bobby Hendricks's melodic 'langarm' (straight-arm) music played in the background. It was a time when 'Boetie Vetvoet' (Uncle Fatfoot) cried 'dronkverdriet' (drunk sadness) as he made his way home from the smokkie down Bream Way.

Even school provided some sanctuary. No matter how dreadful some teachers were, I relished the laughter and chattering voices on the playground. We'd run around the schoolyard, pretending to be serious, budding athletes, and for school sports, we sang our hearts out for our favourite teams. In those moments, I felt free from the gang violence, my father's abuse and the awful teachers.

A few exceptional teachers made school worthwhile. One such teacher was Miss Vink. No matter how dirty or smelly we were, she never criticised us for it. She treated us as if we were her own children and in her class I didn't have to fear being sniffed out as a stinker or a gravedigger or having to recite that stupid line, 'Cleanliness is next to godliness'. The same could be said of Mr and Miss Jansen, brother and sister teachers. They were tall, compassionate giants.

Whereas these teachers were treated with much adoration and respect, the same couldn't be said of how some teachers treated children. Because many of them came from middle-class 'white-coloured' suburbs, it must have frustrated them to spend their days teaching in the squalor of our school, before escaping to the comfort of their homes in the afternoons. Some teachers openly showed affection to kids from 'white' Nooitgedacht. Maybe this made life at school bearable for them. These kids were chosen as favourites: the 'oog appels' (the apples of their eyes).

Such favouritism caused division and created tension. Each of us wanted to be a favourite, an oog appel, so we did whatever we could to win affection. Of course, it wasn't always within our power to do so. You had to be clean, clever, look beautiful or occasionally soothe the teacher with an apple, sandwich or something to win their heart. If you didn't make the cut, there was one loophole left – sport. If you were good at athletics, soccer or rugby, you were in the 'world cup' and your place was secured among the chosen, even if you were from Bream Way or the flats. All you needed to do was perform. But, no matter how hard I tried, I was dismal at sports, so even that option was closed to me. For those who weren't eye apples, it was 'nag' (night), meaning hell was waiting for you.

Take my class teacher, Mr Hendricks, 'die ou boggelrug' (the old hunchback), as we called him. He was forever grumpy and could barely walk upright. He frowned constantly, as if angry with the world for loading its burden onto his back. We might have shown him compassion had it not been for his callous method of dividing the class into clever kids, stupid kids and those who did not fit anywhere. Invariably, most stupid kids were from Bream Way and the flats. Every time I entered his class, I feared landing up in 'domland' (stupidland).

'Here, asseblief, moenie laat ek vandag in domland beland nie,' I'd pray as I entered class. (God, please, don't let me end up in stupidland today.)

Somehow, I always landed up in no-man's land, being neither stupid nor clever. Many never made it out of domland, as was the case with Henrietta, a quiet, nervous girl from Bream Way. Every time Hendricks got to her, he threw up his hands and shouted, 'O, Here Jesus! Hier's ons alweer in domland.' (Oh, Lord Jesus! Here we are again in stupidland.) I don't know how many times I heard that word: Domland! Domland! Domland! I'm sure, if he'd said it to me as many times as he said it to Henrietta, I too would have believed that I was stupid.

Then there was Mr Williams, our physical training teacher. He was athletically built and had straight hair and a 'naaldneus' (needle-nose), which made him popular among the young female teachers. With these attributes, Mr Williams seemed in awe of himself.

One day after school, Francois came home, crying hysterically. 'Mr Williams hit me with his fists and caned me,' he sobbed.

'Why?' my mother asked, distraught.

'I didn't wear my school jersey today because it was dirty.'

My mother was livid. When my father came home that evening, he was so enraged by what had happened to Francois that he took us in his kombi to see the school principal, Mr Hattingh. It was the first time we had journeyed to Glenhaven, a coloured middle-class suburb where the principal lived. We got lost and arrived late. A domestic worker opened the door. My father explained our purpose to her and she made us stand outside for a while, presumably informing the principal of our visit, before allowing us into the house. I'd never been in a house as big and beautiful as that. Every little ornament and decoration had its place. My mother and father were visibly overwhelmed by the environment. I felt out of place.

Once we were inside, the domestic worker escorted us to the lounge and told us to sit. Eventually we heard the principal's voice from somewhere in the passage before he emerged with his big round belly.

'Ja, wat soek julle so laat hier in die nag by my huis?' he yelled, clearly annoyed. (Yes, what are you doing at my house so late at night?)

Francois and I huddled next to my mother, unsure what to expect.

'Goeie naand, meneer Hattingh,' said my father, almost apologetically. 'Ons kom u net sien oor ons kind Francois wat vandag by meneer Williams so ernstig pakgekry het.' (Good evening, Mr Hattingh. We've come to see you about our child Francois, who got such a serious hiding from Mr Williams today.) He then ordered Francois to get up and show Mr Hattingh how the teacher had hit him.

Francois was still in pain, but he dutifully got up, pulled down his pants and showed his buttocks, covered in red marks, to the principal.

The principal turned to my parents and, in a dismissive tone, said, 'Die kinders is stout en dié kind van julle is net so. Jy moet die boompie buig terwyl hy nog klein is.' (The children are naughty and this child of yours is just so. You must bend the tree while he's still young.)

From the expression on their faces, my parents were clearly at a loss and too afraid to challenge the principal's authority. His statement effectively condoned what Mr Williams had done, and on that swift and prompt note, the conversation ended without Francois telling his side of the story.

On our way back, the only sound in the kombi was the engine rattling. The determined expression on my father's face had been replaced by a look of defeat. My mother sat next to him, quietly staring out the windscreen. Who knows what was going through their minds? Francois was quiet, immersed in his own thoughts.

It wasn't the last belittling. Those regarded as problem children bore the brunt of the teachers' brutality, which was deemed corrective discipline. In Standard 3, Francois had a friend named Ashley, a tiny, skinny boy. Mr Onker, a teacher who often came to school drunk, flew into a rage one day and violently assaulted Ashley for a simple mistake. Unable to cope with violence such as this, kids dropped out of school like flies and were absorbed into the swelling ranks of the gangs, to which these teachers had acted as unwitting ushers.

8

A glimmer of hope, a gloom of despair

When I think of life in Bream Way and the flats, Dante's *Inferno* comes to mind. He describes his journey through the nine circles of Hell, accompanied by the Roman poet Virgil. When they get to the Gates of Hell, they are met by this inscription:

> Through me you pass into the city of woe:
> Through me you pass into eternal pain:
> …
> All hope abandon, ye who enter here.

Despite the woe and pain, hell has a way of providing just enough respite to tide you over until your next bout of misery. I passed Standard 5 and was ready to begin high school. Until then, no one in our family had made it to high school except for my mother, who had passed Standard 7. My father had left school at the age of ten when in Standard 1 to work as a cleaner at a bus company.

With my mother pregnant most of the time, Mara had been taken out of school at the age of twelve to help look after us. Francois had failed Standards 1 and 3. By default, I became the pride and joy of our family by going to John Ramsay High School in Bishop Lavis. As a reward, I was given the privilege of a tiny bed in the corner of our small lounge. I was ecstatic: it meant I no longer had to sleep like a sardine, squeezed in between my brothers.

Going to high school was a rite of passage. The first thing you learnt was that the spoon-feeding days of primary school were over. You stepped into a well-oiled machine and had to adjust quickly. In the first year, teachers rotated from one classroom to another, but in the higher grades the pupils changed classrooms for each subject. This was where I got to know some of my teachers better.

Mr Vogt, our history teacher, had a beard and long hippie hair, and often rode to school on his rowdy motorbike. To most pupils, he was the coolest teacher. In class, however, hardly anyone could make sense of what he said. His lessons about the French Revolution were particularly painful. When it came to pronouncing '*Lettres de Cachet*', infamous letters often used by the king of France to imprison his enemies at will without a trial, hardly anyone learnt how to pronounce it. All I heard was something like 'Letter de kassie', a hybrid of Afrikaans and French.

Then there was Ms Griffen, our English teacher, who I really pitied. Struggling against our native Cape Flats Afrikaans, she tried to 'civilise' us with her Queen's English. Our biggest challenge was to pronounce the 'th' in words such as 'thought', 'think' and 'thorough'. Instead, we pronounced them as 'tort', 'tink' and 'taruh'. In the end, our Cape Flats tongues proved too stubborn, refusing to give way to her corrections.

The most memorable of all was Mr Daniels, our Afrikaans teacher. Even though we called him by his surname, everyone knew him as Stinkie, because he always had a bit of yesterday's hangover stink oozing from his body. With his slender form, high cheekbones and short, peperkorrel (peppercorn) hair, you could see the Khoikhoi blood running in his veins. Stinkie was an orator of note. The depth and passion with which he recited works by the great Afrikaans poets such as Totius, C.J. Langenhoven, Eugène Marais and N.P. van Wyk Louw put me in awe of him, even though the poets were Afrikaans. Among them, Eugène Marais stood out, and Stinkie recited the poems 'Winternag' ('O koud is die windjie. En skraal en blink in die dof-lig en kaal') and 'Skoppensboer' (''n Druppel gal is in die soetste wyn; 'n traan is op elk' vrolik' snaar') as if he were Marais himself. Stinkie brought poetry to life.

—ɯ—

High school provided the breathing space I needed. I was happy and enjoyed going, especially when I fell in love with the most beautiful girl in the school.

One day, while playing cricket during lunchbreak, the ball rolled in the direction of the principal's office and I ran after it. That's when I caught a glimpse of her – fair, petite and shy. Her beauty stumped me and I couldn't stop staring. But my adoration was unceremoniously interrupted.

'Charles!' one of my teammates shouted. 'Wat vat djy soe fokken lank? Gooi die fokken bôl.' (Charles! Why the fuck are you taking so long? Throw the fucking ball.)

Annoyed, I threw the ball back to them and continued the game, but I couldn't stop thinking about her.

The following day I was eager to see her again and made periodic sorties to the principal's office, but she was nowhere to be found. For the rest of the week, I walked around the playground, hoping to see her. Just as I was about to give up, I found her standing at the door to the school library with another girl. I didn't have the guts to walk up to her, but I soon found out that her name was Deidre, and she was from Elsies River. Over the next few weeks, I made one excuse after the other not to play cricket so that I could stalk Deidre.

Eventually, I decided to approach her and tell her how beautiful she was. I took hesitant steps until I'd made it to where she and her friend stood. Then disaster struck: I stuttered and couldn't get a word out. The two girls looked at me and burst out laughing. I was so embarrassed that I ran away as quickly as I could.

When my friends found out what had happened, they wouldn't stop teasing me. Initially, I laughed it off, but after a while it was no longer funny.

'Naai, my broe, los daai goose yt, djysie in ha' klasie, my broe,' said my friend Willem. (No, my brother, leave that goose alone, you're not in her class, my brother.)

'Wat bedoel djy?' I asked. (What do you mean?)

'Djy wiet mos. Djy's vannie Bream Way en sy's vannie Elsies.' (You know, man. You're from Bream Way and she's from Elsies.)

I laughed, but I knew exactly what he meant. Willem, like many of us, intuitively espoused the hierarchy of apartheid, which was to know your place in society. Deidre was also coloured, but she stayed in the better part of Elsies River and was fair-skinned, therefore Willem regarded her as a notch or more above me and deemed me unworthy of her. This did not change my feelings towards her, but the dice had been cast. Deidre didn't show any inclination to befriend me.

When I got to Standard 8, most of my mates had girlfriends, making me the odd one out. No one seemed interested in me. Whenever I tried to win a girl's affection, the responses I got, via my friends, were always the same.

'Nie, hy't dik lippe.' (No, he's got thick lips.)

'Sies! Kyk hoe groot en plat is sy nies.' (Gross! Look at how big and flat his nose is.)

'Nie, Got! Hy't a kroeskop.' (No, God! He's got nappy hair.)

I angrily swallowed the comments until I couldn't take them any longer. Bit by bit, they chiselled away at what little self-esteem I had until I began to hate everything about myself: my kroeshare, dik lippe, groot, plat neus and dark-brown skin. I was at war with myself, while also raging at God for having created me this way. Why was I not like the other 'white' kids?

I decided to take matters into my own hands. Sick and tired of my kroeshare, I asked Mara to use her hot iron brush to straighten my hair.

She looked at me in astonishment, her mouth wide open. 'Are you serious?'

'What does it look like?' I replied. 'I'm damn serious.'

Straightening kroeshare was a process. First you washed your hair and prepared it with a relaxer. Wella was the relaxer of choice. A steel comb was heated on a hot plate, and with the hot comb you slowly worked your way through the relaxed hair, always careful not to burn your scalp.

In the opening scene of the movie *Malcolm X*, Malcolm, played by Denzel Washington, has his hair straightened in a method known as conking. As a homemade relaxer is combed through Malcolm's hair, the lye in the mixture starts burning his scalp – a painful but unavoidable part of the conking process. After he is allowed to rinse his hair, Malcolm looks into the mirror and sees a transformed man, one with straight hair. 'Looks white, don't it?' he says, impressed. That's how I felt when Mara was done with me: like a different person.

My best friend, Carlo, was the first to see my new hairstyle. He lived a few streets away and was in a class of his own. Even though his complexion was dark, he had wavy hair that didn't need Wella. What made him stand out was his 'valstande' (false teeth), one of which was gold. He was a winner among the girls and had no difficulty chatting them up. I wanted to be like him and was eager to share in his exploits.

'Ooh! My my! Now we're talking,' he said when he saw my hair. 'Sien djy my valstande met die goue tand? Dis nog wat djy makee. Dan sal djy sien hoe die goese vi' jou val.' (Do you see my false teeth with the gold tooth? That's what you also need. Then you'll see how the girls fall for you.)

It had never occurred to me that one could woo girls by having your four front teeth extracted. I wondered if that was how my father had wooed my mother.

Unbeknown to us, Carlo was prompting me to engage in an age-old practice dating back to the mid-seventeenth century, when Cape Malay slaves removed their front teeth as an act of defiance, symbolically taking back control of their own bodies, which otherwise belonged to their colonial slave masters.

On his advice, I set off to the dentist in Elsies River and, for fifty cents, had all four of my top front teeth extracted. My parents were horrified. Words of admonishment rained down on me that evening and I didn't know where to hide. I was grounded for several weeks and not allowed to see Carlo. Dismayed by the gap in my teeth, my mother eventually gave me money to pay for false teeth. 'No gold tooth,' she warned.

Sporting my new valstande en gladde hare (false teeth and smooth hair) at school, I thought I was the coolest dude around. But no girls showed the slightest interest in me, and Carlo had dropped out of school in favour of a life consumed by alcohol. Stuck with my gladde hare and valstande, I slid all the way down to rock bottom.

9

This madness has to stop

When you're down and out and don't know which way to turn, life forces you to dig a little deeper, and sooner or later you find your way out. I'd lost my sense of self-worth and realised that no amount of 'whiteness' could bring me joy and happiness. This left me feeling like I'd run out of options and had nowhere to turn, but in a bizarre way this meant there was finally a ray of hope on the horizon.

One morning in Standard 9, our mathematics teacher failed to arrive. Instead of behaving like responsible learners, we decided that it was party time. Having had no luck with Deidre or anyone else, I set my sights on the plumpest girl in class and tried to impress her. Together with my friends Roger, Patrick, Bernard and George, I entertained the class with my Michael Jackson antics. Unfortunately, our performance attracted the attention of a teacher, Mr Baartman, who caught us right in the middle of the act. We hurried back to our seats, but he had seen us.

'Julle manne! Kom hier!' he shouted, his face puce. (You guys! Come here!)

Sheepishly, we returned to the front. When he reached for a loose plank on one of the broken benches, my heart sank. I knew what was coming. The class went dead quiet.

'Bernard!' he shouted. I saw the terror in Bernard's eyes as he moved forward. 'Sak, boeta!' (Bend, young man!)

I could barely watch what followed. One! Two! Three! Four! Baartman's wrath fell on Bernard's backside. It didn't take long before he burst into tears. After the sixth stroke Bernard had no more tears left. He just sobbed and endured the pain. By the tenth stroke he was pale and did not utter a word as he crawled back to his seat. The class remained silent.

'Roger! Next!' Baartman shouted. Poor Roger looked at me as if to draw some last-minute strength, but there was nothing I could offer. Baartman ripped into him: One! Two! Three! Four! Five! Six! Seven! Eight! Nine! Ten!

Then, 'Charles!' I felt as if I'd already endured twenty beatings. I stood still for a moment, not knowing what to do, and then moved forward, bent over and stretched out. I closed my eyes. When the first stroke fell, I felt an intense, penetrating pain. As the blows continued to fall, I lost all will to count. By the time it was over, I could hardly walk. I staggered back to my seat and something broke inside me. My heart was drenched in hatred and I didn't shed a tear. *Baartman, jou ma se poes!* I raged inside as I watched him beat George and Patrick.

News of the assault soon spread throughout the school and I was quick to tell Francois. He had since made it to the same high school I attended, but the incident with Mr Williams had hardened his attitude towards teachers. By Standard 8, he was a member of the Student Representative Council (SRC). Its purpose was to represent pupils in grievances about school matters. 'Bastard! Fokken bastard!' he yelled when I told him what had happened. 'Moenie worry nie, djy sal sien wat ek met die vark gaan maak.' (Don't worry, you'll see what I'm going to do with the pig.)

The last time I'd seen Francois fuming like that was a few years earlier, when I came home crying because Barby, the local shop bully, had taken my sweets and hit me. 'Just tell me where he is,' Francois had demanded. On our way back to the shop, I trailed after him like a Chihuahua following a Rottweiler.

Barby was in a jovial mood and didn't notice our arrival. By the time he did, it was too late. Francois pulled him by his T-shirt, punched him a few times in the face and then headbutted him, one, two, three times. As Barby fell to the ground, Francois pummelled him with further blows. The stoep was spattered with blood and Barby's friends stood by, afraid that they too might suffer his fate. When Francois had had enough, he left Barby lying on the stoep. 'Kô' Charles! Laat ôs loep,' he said. (Come Charles! Let's go.) I followed. 'Don't tell Mommy what just happened,' he warned. After that, I had no problems with Barby. I was confident that Francois would sort Baartman out.

An urgent SRC meeting was called to discuss the Baartman incident. Pupils and teachers were enraged, and after heated deliberation, the SRC decided to publish a pamphlet and circulate it to everyone at the school: 'Down with Baartman, Down! Phansi Baartman, Phansi! Away with Baartman, Away!' It was a rallying call for pupils to unite, and they heeded it. They even refused to attend classes, and some teachers openly came out in solidarity with us. The campaign bore fruit and, after a few days, Baartman was no longer seen on the school premises. Francois had successfully taken the anger he harboured against violent teachers and channelled it into school politics.

The incident attracted attention beyond the school and brought an unlikely visitor to our house, a man who set the stage for momentous change in my life. Mr Johnny Bosch was a legendary figure in Bishop Lavis and had often been in police custody for his stand against the apartheid government. My mother politely invited him in when he came to express support for me. He spoke with a carefully articulated English accent, which was unheard of in Nooitgedacht, even among the 'white' coloureds.

'What happened to you at school is the product of gutter education,' he said. 'The system of apartheid has turned us against each other, making us believe that we're inferior and worth nothing. Because of this, some teachers do whatever they want because they, too, believe this to be true; they, too, are products of apartheid's gutter education.'

Never before had someone spoken to us like this. Mr Bosch had all my attention. He went on, telling us about how black people had been divided into different racial groups, making us believe we were different. Yet the same system of Bantu education was applied to all of us, just in different ways.

As he spoke, a realisation dawned and I began to put the pieces together: the school inspector, Hendricks, Williams, Onker, Hattingh and now Baartman. All of these men were products of gutter, Bantu education. Mr Bosch couldn't have come at a better time; amid all the darkness, he'd brought light into our house. Before he left, he gave me a book: *The Crimes of Bantu Education* by Jane Gool. I couldn't wait to retreat to my bed to read it.

The introduction had a riveting heading: 'Mortal blow at the most vulnerable and defenceless – the child'.

Then it began:

Perhaps the greatest crime that can be inflicted on any people is to strike a blow at its youth – the most defenceless. Bantu Education in South Africa does precisely that ... It was designed with only one purpose in view, namely, to deprive the most vulnerable sector of the population – the African child of obtaining a modern, free, and enlightened education.

In his own country, the land of his birth, he will see the magnificent buildings, the well-equipped schools, the spacious lawns, the well-kept playing fields and other amenities but these are not for him. These are for the children of the Herrenvolk (a term commonly used in South Africa to designate the White ruling class). Herrenvolk policy specifically states: 'The education of the White child prepares him for life in a dominant society and the education of the Black child for a subordinate society ... the limits (of Native education) form part of the social and economic structure.'

What I was reading made my blood rush, but I carried on.

Thus the African child born in a society which designates him as an inferior human being, must be taught in a manner to fit him to take his position in that society as an inferior ... After a decade of this debased education it is possible to see the heavy toll it has taken and the inroads it has made on those institutions that had formerly set an example to the whole of Africa for its comparatively advanced system of education. The bitter price that the African child has to pay and is paying today will be felt for generations after.

When I finished reading the introduction that evening, I was befok (livid). It all made sense – the school inspector telling me not to aim too high; Mr Hendriks's 'domland' antics; some teachers' stupid obsession with cleanliness being next to godliness; the principal's arrogant assertion that one must 'buig die boompie terwyl hy nog klein is' (bend the sapling while he is still young); and the savagery meted out by the likes of Williams, Onker and Baartman. These were all attempts at striking that mortal blow at the vulnerable African child. As I lay in my bed, mulling over what I'd read, I cursed the lot, but left my venom for the grand architect of Bantu education: 'Hendrik Verwoerd! Jou ma se poes!' It felt good. That evening, I slept very well.

The following day I couldn't wait to get home from school.

'Mara! Mara!' I shouted. 'How quick can you turn my straight hair into an afro again?'

Stunned and puzzled, she looked at me and then turned away. I got the message: there was nothing I could do but wait for my afro to grow again. Which it did. I had never thought the day would come when I'd look in the mirror and feel good about myself, but soon I smiled at my lovely kroeshare, touched my plat neus with its groot, breë neusgate, stroked my dik lippe, and was proud of my beautiful, brown skin.

10

The flames stir like beckoning hands

In 1985, we sat in the grip of our black-and-white television set. Week in and week out, we jockeyed for the best positions, not to watch *Dallas*, which was popular at the time, but for footage of tyres burning in townships across South Africa. The world's spotlight turned on the country as one township after the other went up in flames – Alexandra, Sebokeng, Bonteheuwel, Bishop Lavis, Athlone, Gugulethu, Soweto, Atteridgeville, Katlehong, Mamelodi, Tembisa, Vosloorus … to name but a few. Like Marais's grass plumes in his poem 'Winternag', the flames stirred like beckoning hands across the country.

Our streets were patrolled by military vehicles that looked as if they'd rolled off a B-grade alien movie set. My mother went from praying about the Josters and Flat Boys to praying about the Casspirs outside. 'Here! Beskerm ons tog asseblief teen hierdie duiwelse Casspirs hier buite.' (God! Please protect us against these devilish Casspirs outside.) My father's tune was different: 'Julle politiek en politiek! Julle moet ophou met die politiek.' (You politick and politick! You must stop with the politicking.) But Francois and I couldn't.

The Williams and Baartman incidents had propelled Francois to the forefront of school politics. Other pupils too were gatvol (fed up) with apartheid, and rejected Verwoerd's Bantu education. They no longer accepted what teachers taught them, but questioned, engaged and, where necessary, defied. Mr Vogt was quick to respond. He stopped following the official, sanitised Afrikaner curriculum that justified apartheid, and openly taught the history of banned organisations: the African National Congress (ANC) and the Pan Africanist Congress (PAC), and their leaders Nelson Mandela, Robert Sobukwe and the

Black Consciousness advocate Stephen Bantu Biko. Even Stinkie began to recite Cape Flats poems such as 'Die Here het gaskommel' (The Lord threw dice) by Adam Small and 'Ek is oek important' (I am also important) by Peter Snyders.

It was also time for pupils to settle old scores, and the woodwork teacher, Mr Cupido, was the first target. Everyone knew him as 'Jumbo', because he was so fat that he shuffled. Jumbo knew we poked fun at him behind his back, and his response was to throw five-pound hammers, chisels and try squares at us – anything he could lay his hands on.

One day, Jumbo had unexpectedly shuffled into our classroom and caught Ruby, a red-haired, freckle-faced girl, chatting loudly to a friend. Jumbo fumed and laid into Ruby: 'Hey! Djy! Met daai fokken klomp vlieëkak in jou gesig. Hou jou fokken bek.' (Hey! You! With all that fucking fly shit on your face. Shut your fucking mouth.)

Ruby burst into tears, and Jumbo shuffled back to his classroom.

Athol Williams, one of Francois's friends and a fellow SRC representative, had it in for Jumbo. Rumour had it that one morning, Athol marched into Jumbo's classroom and ordered all learners to leave the class. Then he calmly walked up to Jumbo, looked him in the eyes and, with all the hatred and disgust he'd built up over the years, spat in his face and said, 'Jou ma se poes.' With that, Athol calmly left the classroom. Jumbo said nothing. Pupils rejoiced, because as disgusting as the incident was, the teacher had had it coming.

The year 1985 was to me what 1976 was to those who participated in the student uprising. It brought thousands of us onto the streets armed only with stones and tyres. At school, every time we heard the signal 'Casspir', we'd go befok and storm out of our classes to take up positions alongside the advance scouts, whose task it was to watch for Casspirs from the school's front gates. They were the brave and adventurous ones, although they also used the opportunity to bunk classes. Francois and the other student leaders strategised and planned the course of protest action. They engaged teachers and the principal, called mass meetings and decided when classes would be interrupted.

During this time, two movements emerged at school – those who believed in education before liberation and those who supported the call for liberation before education. Francois belonged to the latter group, who were influenced by the 1976 student uprising and were prepared to risk it all for the sake of liberation. But his stance pitted him against his namesake, Francois Groepe.

Groepe was 'die mees voorbeeldige skoolseun' (the most exemplary schoolboy) who took his schoolwork very seriously. He was an ardent supporter of education before liberation, whereas Francois wanted Bantu education abolished and replaced. Groepe believed pupils had to work within the system, and urged them to return to class. While most teachers scorned Francois and adored Groepe, most pupils were distrustful of Groepe's exemplary ways.

Not only was I faced with choosing between these two extremes, but my mother's anguish deeply troubled me too. 'Ai, my kind,' she sighed, 'ek hoop jy gaan matriekeksamens skryf en die familie trots maak.' (Oh, my child, I hope you're going to write matric exams and make the family proud.) This put me in an existential crisis – to write or not to write? To write meant making the family proud as its first matriculant, but turning my back on the call to boycott the matric exams. Worse, I had to choose between my mother and my brother. Fortunately, the answer became clear early one morning when there was a frantic knocking on our front door. Thinking it was someone who needed my father's help, I opened the door, and in stormed white and coloured policemen armed with machine guns, shouting, 'Is jy Francois Abrahams? Ons soek vir Francois!' (Are you Francois Abrahams? We're looking for Francois!)

Before I could utter a word, my parents were in the lounge, having been woken by the noise.

'Wat gaan aan? Wat soek julle hier?' my mother yelled. (What's going on? What are you doing here?) At the time, she was pregnant with Lorenzo.

'Ons is hier vir Francois Abrahams,' responded a tall white policeman. (We are here for Francois Abrahams.) He introduced himself as Captain Laubscher.

Francois appeared before they could search the house. 'I'm Francois,' he said in a cool, calm voice, as if he'd known that his political activism would lead to his arrest.

'Ons kom om jou te arresteer,' said the captain. (We've come to arrest you.)

When my mother heard those words, she broke down in tears. My father went on like a fool: 'Ek het mos gesê julle moet ophou met die politiek, maar julle wil nie hoor nie. Kyk nou waar het dit julle gekry.' (I told you to stop with the politics, but you didn't want to listen. Now look where you've landed up.)

Once Francois had gathered some clothes, they escorted him to a police vehicle, where a contingent of police and military personnel waited for him. I held back my tears while I comforted my mother. 'Don't worry, Mommy, he's strong. He'll be okay.' I had no idea where they would take him, though. Meanwhile, my father left for work without saying a word.

That morning, news of the arrest spread across the school. Some teachers and other SRC leaders had also been arrested. It was chaos. Pupils were reluctant to go to class; they wanted action. With many of the SRC's leadership arrested, we looked to those left behind: Athol Williams, who'd allegedly spat in Jumbo's face; Mario Byneveldt, whose brother was also involved in student politics; Eric Alam, who was just gatvol with the system; Fergus Pienaar, the head boy who wanted to lead by example; Allen Aubrey, who always had transport; and me. With Francois incarcerated, how could I not step forward and lead the pupils? An injury to one was an injury to all.

With the matric exams close at hand, the question of whether to write or boycott had turned into a highly personal and political issue. On the morning of the first exam, a number of Casspirs arrived at school along with a heavy presence of gun-toting police and army personnel. Their purpose was to transport pupils to the examination centre. One by one, those matrics who had opted to write sheepishly made their way into the Casspirs. The rest of us watched from the school's parking lot.

Once the Casspirs had gone, we jumped into action. A huge protest gathering was to take place in Athlone, and we planned to attend. In anticipation, we'd prepared pamphlets to honour our teachers and fellow pupils who'd been arrested and detained. Allen Aubrey had secured a car; the rest of us packed it to capacity and we set off in a buoyant mood.

We drove along Lavis Drive before turning into Modderdam Road (now Robert Sobukwe Road). From where I sat, squashed in the back seat, I noticed that Allen kept looking in his rear-view mirror. I didn't make much of it until he said, 'Guys, we've got company.' I knew then that we had trouble; it could only be the police.

'Carry on driving. Don't look around,' said Eric nervously.

I thought about all the pamphlets on my lap and started to sweat, frantically searching for places to hide them – under the front seats, under the carpets, wherever I could find a hole. But our big worry was the pamphlets in the boot.

Just as we were about to turn onto the highway, the police siren went off. 'Pull off! Pull off!' a voice commanded. Allen brought the vehicle to a stop. Everyone was quiet, not knowing what to do or expect. The police cautiously approached the car and ordered us out. Passing vehicles slowed down to see what was going on.

'Waarheen is julle op pad? Is julle nie veronderstel om in die skool te wees nie?' (Where are you off to? Are you not supposed to be at school?)

We looked at each other, not knowing what to say, but before anyone could reply, they discovered the pamphlets. 'See what we've got here!' It was game over: we were arrested and taken to Manenberg Police Station, where I encountered the same Captain Laubscher who had arrested Francois a few days earlier.

'Bingo!' he shouted when he saw me. 'My day is made. I should have arrested you when I arrested your brother. It would have made my work easier.'

They detained us for the night, then took us to Victor Verster Prison in Paarl. From the time we set foot in Victor Verster, it felt as if we'd arrived at one big family gathering. Young and old hugged us warmly. 'Welcome, comrades! Welcome!' they shouted as we made our way with our prison blankets into a huge communal cell of about fifty detainees. The atmosphere was euphoric and comradely and didn't feel like prison at all. Instead, it felt as if everyone was on some compulsory break from street protests.

I settled down beside a bearded detainee a few years older than me, who introduced himself as Cassiem Christians from Mitchells Plain. He was quiet and looked as if he wouldn't hurt a fly. In a soft voice, he told me that the police had arrested him merely for having a stone in his hand. I felt sorry for him.

Later that day, we mingled with other detainees in the forecourt. Big student and activist names like Trevor Manuel, Cecil Esau and Christmas Tinto were there, some with us and others in isolation. As I walked around, I heard a familiar voice shouting, 'Charles! Charles!' And there was Francois, running in my direction. 'Wat maak djy hier?' he shouted. (What are you doing here?) We hugged and spent the rest of the day together.

If ever P.W. Botha, then president of South Africa, did anything that had good consequences, it was bringing all of us together in one place. Victor Verster became a gathering of activists from different political persuasions, where ideas were exchanged amid heated discussions, while some plotted the way forward. In one corner you had the ANC-aligned groups or the Charterists, as they were called (after the Freedom Charter), while in another corner were those from the Azanian People's Organisation (AZAPO) and the PAC-aligned groups, known as the Africanists. In between, you had the smaller groups, such as the African People's Democratic Union of Southern Africa (APDUSA), the Non-European Unity Movement (NEUM) and the New Unity Movement (NUM). Some referred to the smaller groups as the armchair politicians, because they churned out Marxist–Leninist or Trotskyist ideas, but contributed little to political action.

With too little time to fully appreciate each political organisation's ideas and programmes, I moved from one corner to the other, listening attentively to the rigorous debates on the ANC's Freedom Charter, AZAPO's Azanian Manifesto and APDUSA's Ten-Point Programme. These impassioned debates led to the occasional blow-up, and each group was eager to recruit young blood like me into their camp while warning me away from others. 'Don't spend too much time with Cassiem,' a Charterist told me. 'He belongs to a radical Muslim group.' During a violent protest, so the story went, the police had entered a mosque looking for fleeing activists. Outraged by the desecration of the sacred space, Cassiem and his comrades had opened fire with heavy automatic rifles. I couldn't believe that soft-spoken Cassiem was capable of doing that. When I confronted him about it, he just smiled and cautioned me not to believe what others said.

Even though I never joined any of the political organisations, I was impressed by the intellectual rigour and astuteness of the smaller groups, as they mostly outdid the bigger movements in political debates. But I was more attracted to the pragmatism of the established forma- tions at the forefront of the struggle.

After two weeks, I was released. When I stepped out, I felt energised and invigorated, ready for the next battle. But back at home, a more familiar kind of politics awaited me. My mother had given birth to Lorenzo and my father was spending even more time at church. The wedge between them had grown bigger and the house was in turmoil, heading for an implosion. Most of the time, my eight younger siblings were at each other's throats, shouting, screaming and fighting, while the little ones cried for attention. I refereed where I could, separated those in conflict, and pandered to the smaller ones. My mother was a physical and emotional wreck and barely had the energy to care for Lorenzo. Francois was held in detention for another two months, and I found myself unwillingly in charge of Bream Way's sinking *Titanic*. What a welcome back.

11

The dust settles

By January 1986, the fires of rebellion had died in Nooitgedacht and the surrounding areas. The streets were quiet, as many students and activists lingered in detention. The south-easter blew lightly, and even though it was summer, there was a chill in the air. Except for the occasional faint cry of a small child, Bream Way was silent. Children were back at school and factories had reopened in mid-January.

Aunty Dotty, our opposite neighbour, emerged from her maisonette and walked towards her front gate. Standing with legs astride, she looked down the street, hawked up a load of phlegm and spat. 'Enna! Jou fokken tief! Kom hie!' she yelled at her eldest daughter. (Enna! You fucking bitch! Come here!)

'Fok jou! Wie's jou fokken tief!' Enna responded from down the road. (Fuck you! Who's your fucking bitch!)

A stray dog ran towards the overflowing sewage drain outside our house to quench its thirst. Only my mother, Mara and I were at home.

'Wat nou? Wat gaan jy doen?' my mother asked me as she and Mara cleaned the house. (What now? What are you going to do?)

My schooldays were over, even though I'd boycotted the matric exams. For the first time in twelve years, I'd woken up not knowing what to do with myself.

'Why don't you find a job? Everyone does so after school,' my mother suggested.

'A job!' I stared at her, annoyed at the very idea.

It was normal for young men and women from Nooitgedacht, Bishop Lavis and Valhalla Park to work as manual labourers at the nearby warehouses and factories servicing the airport.

'No, Mommy,' I protested. 'I want to study, no matter what, even if it means having to repeat my matric year.'

She interrupted her cleaning, looked at me and then relented without saying a word.

Fortunately, the education department afforded those who'd not written their final matric examinations an opportunity to sit for the supplementary examinations in March. To my surprise, many of my schoolmates who had written the matric exams sat the supplementary exams. Not even the Casspir protection had helped them through the first time. Too embarrassed to greet me when I arrived at the venue, most kept their heads bowed, pretending to be immersed in last-minute preparation. The exams went well and I was anxious for the results.

The events of 1985 had dulled the atmosphere at home. Francois hadn't been able to write his Standard 9 exams and had no intention of going back to school. Shortly after his release from detention, he confided in me that he intended to leave the country and join the banned PAC in exile. It came as a shock. My intuitive response was to dissuade him as I couldn't imagine being without my brother and pillar of support. Going into exile also meant potentially taking up arms against the apartheid government and placing your life at risk. But his mind was made up. 'I don't have a future in this country,' he said. I wasn't surprised by his choice of liberation movement. As children, my mother often told us stories of PAC founder Robert Sobukwe, who was born in Graaff-Reinet, not too far from Aberdeen in the Eastern Cape, where she was born. We decided not to tell our parents about Francois's decision.

I had different plans. I'd long since moved on from my childhood dream of wanting to be a heart surgeon, and now I wanted to go to university and study law. Since reading Jane Gool, I was incensed by the gross injustices of apartheid, and becoming a lawyer felt like the right thing to do. I had my sights on the University of the Western Cape (UWC), not too far from where we lived. I'd often heard students refer to it as 'bush' and thought it was because of its location in the bushy Modderdam area. Only later did I discover that it was a derogatory term in response to the apartheid government, which had established the university in 1959 to provide inferior tertiary education to 'coloured' students. Over the years, however, UWC had become a hotbed of political activity and attracted many anti-apartheid activists.

By late March, the university was still open for registration, but I hadn't yet received my matric results. On the last day of registration, I decided to take a chance and try to register without my results. With no money for taxi fare, I ran the five kilometres to UWC in sweltering heat. When I got there, sweaty and exhausted, I had to join a long registration queue. Two hours later, I finally got to the registration desk, only to have the clerk tell me, 'No matric results, no registration.'

I begged, but to no avail, and left the university feeling miserable. With the last bit of energy left in me, I took the road back home.

When I stepped into the house, my mother was excited. 'Your results have just come. You passed!' she thrilled. I couldn't believe it. I took the letter from her and collapsed onto the sofa, breathing heavily. They weren't the best of results – two Ds, four Es and an F – but it was a pass nonetheless. By then, it was already after 4 p.m. I had no energy left to run back to the university, and even if I had, it would have been closed.

In the days that followed, I thought long and hard about what to do next. Jane Gool's book and the events of 1985 had made me restless. I wanted to know more about the world around me and my place in it, and I wanted to understand the big political and economic ideas such as capitalism, socialism and communism I'd heard so much about during my detention. I wanted to know why I was poor and labelled 'coloured'. I feared that Bantu education may already have blighted my capacity to comprehend all of these things. With university out of the question for now, I decided on a plan that seemed preposterous at first, even to me: I would educate myself in each of these matters, ranging from politics and economics to religion and philosophy. My English was dreadful, so I would need to brush up on it. This self-education would be a colossal task, but I was determined to do it. In detention, I'd learnt that Karl Marx, father of communism, had spent much of his time in the British Museum writing *Das Kapital*. If he could do it, so could I. I decided to spend a year of my life educating myself in the Cape Town Central Library.

My decision didn't go down well with my parents, especially my father. 'It's a waste of money!' he yelled at me. 'You should go work.' My mother remained silent. I knew my decision would cause my family further hardship, but I was resolute. My mother grudgingly agreed to pay for my weekly train ticket to Cape Town, leaving her with less money for food, but I couldn't wait for my first day at the library.

12

The road less travelled

At the Cape Town Central Library, the first thing I did was lay my hands on Marx's *Capital*, Volume One. I was surprised to find it on the shelf, considering its association with communism, the biggest ideological enemy of the apartheid state. I grabbed it with both hands and made my way to the reading room. I'd never read a book so thick, but after some procrastination, I got going.

> The wealth of societies in which the capitalist mode of production prevails appears as an 'immense collection of commodities' ... The commodity is ... an external object, a thing which through its qualities satisfies human needs ... The usefulness of a thing makes it a use value.

I had not expected *Capital* to start off on such a complex and incomprehensible note. It was nowhere close to the easy, emotive Marxist slogans I was used to: 'Workers of the world unite; you have nothing to lose but your chains.' Or 'Revolutions are the locomotives of history', and 'The history of all previous societies has been the history of class struggles.' I hadn't thought I'd be confronted with an analysis of the use and exchange values of commodities.

Still hopeful, I soldiered on, but then gave up a few pages later. 'Fok,' I muttered. 'This is no book for working-class people. It's too intellectual.' *Capital* was intimidating, making me feel stupid and like an arse. Overwhelmed, I took a break and walked to the window overlooking the Grand Parade.

There was the usual hustle and bustle 'oppie Parara' (on the Parade), with the flea market in full swing. 'Five bob! Five bob!' (Fifty cents! Fifty cents!) a fruit seller shouted in the distance, followed by, 'Hie's jou geluk! Hie's jou geluk!' (Here's your luck! Here's your luck!) Close by, pigeons graced the statue of King Edward VII with their droppings. I stared out for a short while before returning to the shelves to find something easier. Some Marx-for-beginners book came to hand; exactly what I needed.

I spent the rest of the day reading and making copious notes. Time ticked by, one hour after the other, as people came and went. Before I knew it, the day was over and it was time to head home. Reading had been a satisfying experience and I was thirsting for more, so going to the library became a routine.

In the morning, I got up at 6 a.m., washed, dressed, packed my bag and headed for the train station. At that hour, workers were making their way to the station in Bishop Lavis. More people joined the throng along the way, some wearing blue overalls, others carrying the tools of their trade. Women wore kopdoekies (headscarves) and clutched their handbags tightly. By the time we reached the open field close to the station, there were hundreds of us, and some picked up the pace to secure a place in the packed trains.

On the platform, it was mayhem. The ticket controllers were outnumbered and simply gave way to the passengers. Scuffles ensued as passengers shoved each other to get into the train. 'Moenie mol 'ie! Moenie mol 'ie!' (Don't push! Don't push!) some shouted, but to no avail. I joined the fray and pushed my way through the crowd until I got into a carriage. By the time the whistle had blown and the train started moving, passengers were still trying to board while others hung out of the doors. Inside, there was hardly room to breathe. I stood with my bag against sweaty, foul-smelling bodies. 'Djarre, working class!' I giggled. Next stop was Bonteheuwel and then Langa. A few people got off, but many more forced their way on.

As the train made its way to the next station, someone started to sing, 'Hosanna! Hosanna! … Ôs ga hemel toe … wanner Jesus kom.' (Hosanna! Hosanna! … We're going to heaven … when Jesus comes.) Others joined in. Then the singer began preaching: 'Halleluja! Mense!

Julle moet julle bekeer wan die koms vannie Here is naby!' (Hallelujah! People! You must repent because the coming of Christ is near!) People listened in attentive silence. I listened too, but with an awareness of inner conflict. Given my own upbringing in a handeklapkerkie, a part of me intuitively latched on to the sermon, but my newfound rational, intellectual experience suppressed it. Another hymn followed the sermon.

The train arrived in Pinelands, where well-dressed men and women, many of them 'white' coloureds, alighted from first class with their briefcases. This was where Old Mutual, one of South Africa's largest insurance companies, had its head office. Next were Maitland and Paarden Island, two industrial stops where mostly blue-collared men got off. Then Salt River, the hub of the garment factories, followed by Woodstock, home of the fish factory Irvin & Johnson. Here, the women with the kopdoekies got off. With the train almost empty, it finally entered Cape Town station, where I was headed. Over time, this route gave me a glimpse into the lives of working-class people in transit, and I felt like one of them.

During my several months in the library, philosophy, politics, economics and religion came to life for me, and I developed close relationships with the works of famous philosophers and world-renowned leaders. I decided to focus on the Greek philosophers to learn how to understand and interpret the world. I was impressed that they'd rejected the myths of earlier civilisations in favour of empirical evidence (information gained from experience or observation) and rationality (being able to argue logically, whether empirically based or not). This way of thinking led to what is generally referred to as the scientific approach, which today constitutes the bedrock of Western thought.

One might have expected the Greeks' rationality to affirm their belief in the world as primary and disavow their belief in the existence of gods, but Plato, one of the greatest Greek philosophers, believed that the physical, sensory world was less real than the eternal and intelligible world that existed beyond the physical world. This eternal world, he believed, could only be perceived through rigorous education. Plato also held that the beauty and order of the universe was created by a rational, purposive and beneficent god, a 'demiurge', who worked in the public interest. This god apparently ordered the world out of chaos and organised it into the four elements of earth, water, air and fire, which constitute the body of the universe, while the recurring circular motion of the sun, moon, planets and stars made up the soul.

I was intrigued that Plato believed in a god despite being a rationalist. Curious to understand whether one could retain one's faith in the Christian God and still be a rationalist, I turned again to Marx, an avowed atheist and rationalist who'd outright rejected the idea of a god as meaningless in a rational world.

I struggled to fully comprehend their ideas, but nevertheless immersed myself in Marx's and Plato's contrasting world views as the days went by. Because I'd grown up in a religious house where faith held sway, I experienced Marx's views as an epiphany that shattered my beliefs. 'Religious suffering is, at one and the same time, the expression of real suffering and a protest against real suffering. Religion is the sigh of the oppressed creature, the heart of a heartless world, and the soul of soulless conditions. It is the opium of the people,' Marx held.

This made sense to me, and in contrast I found it difficult to believe that Plato's god was working in the public interest. After all, my own miserable childhood included being beaten and disparaged by teachers who'd used religion to justify abuse, and I'd watched my father beat my mother, despite him being a deeply devout Christian. An even bigger reason to embrace Marx's views on religion and reject Plato's was the way religion had been used to con South Africans into believing that apartheid was the natural order. As a child, I'd been taught that the triumph of Afrikaner whites over the powerful Zulu king Dingane at the Battle of Blood River on 16 December 1838 was the fulfilment of a solemn covenant with God, who'd apparently delivered them from the Zulus. This day became known as the Day of the Vow (now Reconciliation Day).

I discovered that, like the Old Testament Israelites, the Afrikaners believed they enjoyed a special relationship with God, which the first apartheid prime minister, D.F. Malan, described in colourful terms:

Our history is the greatest masterpiece of the centuries. We hold this nationhood as our due for it was given to us by the Architect of the Universe. [His] aim was the formation of a new nation among the nations of the world ... The last one hundred years have witnessed a miracle behind which must lie a divine plan. Indeed, the history of the Afrikaner reveals a will and a determination which makes one feel that Afrikanerdom is not the work of men but the creation of God.

With their roots firmly established in divine authority, Afrikaner theologians believed that apartheid was the will of God. They found justification for the subjugation and control of the 'heathen' black majority in the biblical scripture in which God vested the Israelites with authority:

When the Lord your God brings you into the land you are entering to possess and drives out before you many nations ... and when the Lord your God has delivered them over to you and you have defeated them, then you must destroy them totally. Make no treaty with them, and show them no mercy. (Deuteronomy 7:1–2)

Armed with Marx's ideas, I had ample reason to doubt the existence of God and terminate my faith in him. Even if God existed, I was now convinced he was a vengeful, biased and jealous God. He may have sided with the oppressed Israelites, yet he also emboldened them to oppress those who either were not his chosen or didn't believe in him. No wonder Afrikaners readily relied on God to justify apartheid.

But the decision to let go wasn't easy. For weeks, I wrestled with myself. As contradictory as it was, religion provided most of the basic values instilled in my life: 'Be kind towards others. Do unto them as you wish they would do to you' (Luke 6:31); 'Don't be selfish. Be humble' (Philippians 2:3).

I found a way out through the similarity between Marx's thought and the Christian concept of salvation. Both located their preordained societies in the future – Marx's classless, communist society and Christianity's New Jerusalem. Both had their 'uitverkorenes' (the elect): for Marx, it was the working class, and for Christians, its faithful believers. Both invoked conflict to achieve their end goal – the working class would overthrow the bourgeois, capitalist class through revolution, and Christians were engaged in an ongoing spiritual battle against Satan, which would come to a head with Jesus Christ's Second Coming and his defeat of Satan.

I tried to make light of the similarities during my early-morning train journeys as I listened differently to the preacher's sermons. They were like Marxist sermons, but spiritual. Now and then, I joined the fray, crying 'Hallelujah! Amen!' alongside the workers. I decided to accept Marx's material world as real, but a part of me retained my belief in Plato's intelligible world. In grappling with these concerns, my intellectual confidence had grown. It was liberating to discover that the world was a deeply contested place of ideas and that no single set reigned supreme. My mind felt free, light and unshackled from the weight of the clutter that had burdened it. I hungered for knowledge and roamed around the library as if it were my own little university. My English improved, too.

I crossed into other disciplines, such as economics. My rudimentary understanding of scarcity, supply and demand, productivity and economic output helped me develop a basic understanding of how the apartheid economy functioned, such as its reliance on the supply of cheap black labour to the gold mines in Johannesburg and the Free State. Gold was the lifeline to forms of domestic and international credits that maintained the apartheid regime. I was interested in those who'd bankrolled apartheid, but couldn't find much material on it. Instead, I stumbled upon an eccentric economist with some interesting ideas: Karl Polanyi. In *The Great Transformation*, Polanyi argued that international finance served as the main link between political and economic organisations, and could function as an instrument for global peace but also finance wars. I couldn't help but wonder what role international finance played in maintaining the system of apartheid.

But I chose not to take my library research any further for now. Marx, Plato and other European philosophers had provided me with an understanding of the larger world, but not with the world in which I was living. I hoped to find these answers at the offices of the South African Committee for Higher Education (SACHED) Trust, which housed a rich collection of contemporary African political writings. So, with only a few months to go before the end of the year, I brought my time in the library to an end. I was sad that I had to leave the place that had become a second home to me – the books, the philosophers and their ideas. I would miss the daily commute with the preachers and workers on the crammed, smelly trains, and the reading experience that had begun to transform my outlook on the world. But I was also happy to move on.

SACHED was based in Mowbray, and instead of a train ride, I caught a minibus taxi in Modderdam Road. I adapted to a different rhythm. 'Nou ry! Gou ry!' the gaatjie (taxi guard) would shout as I crossed the road and ran for the taxi. Like the train, it was packed and stuffy, but the passengers were quiet, less engaged.

I'd already befriended some of the helpful staff at SACHED, but it was my introduction to its director, Dr Neville Alexander, that cemented my hunger for intellectual contemplation. He had spent a decade on Robben Island in the 1960s and 1970s as a political prisoner, and some called him a political assassin. Others considered him an intellectual guerrilla, but to most he was a renowned linguist, academic and activist.

I met Alexander shortly after reading his book, *Sow the Wind*. His views on race fascinated me at a time when the fight against apartheid attracted both multi-racialists and non-racialists. Despite their calls for racial equality, one couldn't tell whether the multi-racialists believed in race based on biological grounds or rooted in social ideas. To Alexander, race had no valid biological basis. According to him, even Hitler, in 1934, was reported to have said:

I know very well that in a scientific sense there is no such thing as race. As a politician, however, I need a concept that makes it possible to destroy the historical bases that have existed hitherto and to put in their place a completely new and anti-historical 'order' and to give to this new order an intellectual basis.

Alexander squarely aligned himself with the 'lumpers', the no-race theorists, who he believed were on the strategic offensive against the 'splitters', the many-races theorists. He believed it was only a matter of time before the splitters put up the white flag. I aligned myself with Alexander's views.

As I worked my way through the contemporary African collection, I came across the works of Kwame Nkrumah, Julius Nyerere, Patrice Lumumba, Amílcar Cabral, Frantz Fanon and many more. As I had thrilled to the works of Plato and Marx, so I was taken to a new high by these African leaders who represented a new spirit of freedom, independence and Pan-Africanism. Nkrumah, independence leader of Ghana, announced the birth of a new African personality and identity in his speech on 6 March 1957 (the day Ghana became independent from Britain): 'Today, from now on, there is a new African in the world. That African is ready to fight his own battle … We are going to create our own African personality and identity.' But as Nkrumah was a Pan-Africanist at heart, he also stated, 'Our independence is meaningless unless it's linked up to the total independence of the African continent.'

Nyerere, Lumumba and Cabral, independence leaders of Tanzania, the Republic of the Congo and Guinea-Bissau respectively, followed suit. But it was Steve Biko, South Africa's Black Consciousness leader, whose identity politics made the biggest impression on me. I felt a greater personal connection to Biko's ideas than I had to those of Marx, Plato and other European philosophers, and his Black Consciousness provided the philosophical, moral and political pieces missing in my lived experience. Skimming through some of his writings, I saw that Biko lashed out at black politicians, whether African, coloured or Indian, who'd succumbed to apartheid's race-based ideology and practised narrow black-identity politics. 'Xhosas want their Transkei, the Zulus their Zululand etc.,' he chastised Kaiser Matanzima and Chief Mangosuthu Buthelezi. 'They accept that the rest of South Africa is for whites ... none of them sees himself as fighting the battle for all black people.'

But it was Biko's observations about coloured people that proved decisive and provided the answer to years of struggle with my own coloured identity. 'Coloured people harbour secret hopes of being classified as "brown Afrikaners" and therefore meriting admittance into the white laager.' In this one sentence, Biko pinpointed the source of my childhood identity troubles – believing that my coloured skin was worthless and that I should aspire to be white. His views were the tool I needed to dig deeper. If race had no biological validity, it baffled me that an entire social group could, almost wholesale, deny its own identity. It didn't take me long before I found the answer.

A little book locked in a glass cabinet had caught my attention. When the soft-spoken librarian handed it to me, I couldn't let go of it. It was Frantz Fanon's seminal work, *Black Skin, White Masks*. It read like a sequel to Biko's views on race. The Afro-Caribbean psychiatrist and philosopher explored the deep emotional and psychological dimensions that colonialism had left in its wake and foreshadowed the problems faced by Africans seeking to forge a new identity and personality.

[E]very colonized people – in other words, every people in whose soul an inferiority complex has been created by the death and burial of its local cultural originality – finds itself face to face with the language of the civilizing nation; that is, with the culture of the mother country. The colonized is elevated above his jungle status in proportion to his adoption of the mother country's cultural standards. He becomes whiter as he renounces his blackness, his jungle.

After observing the behaviour and attitudes of Antillean and Martinique men influenced by colonial French culture, Fanon mockingly portrayed them in an almost court-jester fashion.

The black man who has lived in France ... returns radically changed. To express it in genetic terms, his phenotype undergoes a definitive, an absolute mutation. Even before he had gone away, one could tell from the almost aerial manner of his carriage that new forces had been set in motion. When he met a friend or an acquaintance, his greeting was no longer the wide sweep of the arm: With great reserve our 'new man' bowed slightly. The habitually raucous voice hinted at a gentle inner stirring as of rustling breezes.

Biko's observation of coloured people had served as a cursory diagnosis of an age-old colonial disease, but Fanon's account was in-depth. It sliced through my being like a surgeon's scalpel and by the time I got to read his next important work, *The Wretched of the Earth*, I knew I was in for extensive identity surgery. Fanon brought home the immense psychological impact apartheid had had on me:

> Because it is a systematic negation of the other person and a furious determination to deny the other person all attributes of humanity, colonialism forces the people it dominates to ask themselves the question constantly: 'In reality, who am I?'

I knew I had a tough task in trying to overcome years of Bantu education and apartheid indoctrination. And as hopeful as I was about Nkrumah's African identity politics and Biko's Black Consciousness, these ideas were under siege. Hardly three months into his term as prime minister of the Congo, Lumumba was arrested in a coup. Four months later, in January 1961, he was executed by a firing squad and replaced by the Congo's most vicious and brutal dictator, Mobutu Sese Seko. The United States Central Intelligence Agency (CIA) and the governments of Britain and Belgium were fingered in the coup. On 24 February 1966, while on a trip to China and Vietnam, Nkrumah was deposed in a bloody coup back home. Later, declassified documents revealed that the CIA had again played a role. And if that wasn't enough, Amílcar Cabral was assassinated in 1973 with the help of Portuguese intelligence.

Biko, too, was murdered. On the morning of 17 August 1977, he and fellow Black Consciousness leader Peter Jones travelled from the Eastern Cape to Cape Town for a series of meetings with their fellow leaders. On their return to the Eastern Cape, they were stopped at a roadblock outside King William's Town and taken to separate police stations. Over the next twenty days, Biko was stripped, manacled and tortured until he sustained a brain haemorrhage. On 12 September 1977, after being driven naked in a police van for more than seven hundred kilometres to Pretoria, he died in police custody. His death was poorly covered up as a hunger strike.

What struck me about these horrific deaths was the sudden and unexpected manner in which they occurred. Clearly, the very idea of an independent African and Black Consciousness identity constituted a threat to the former colonial, white interests. Black thought and ideas would therefore be suppressed at all costs. As unnerving as this was, I was too deep into identity politics to give it up and I refused to back off from my quest to find my own African identity.

13

Barefoot to the home
of the democratic intellectual

In 1987, university beckoned. My application to study law at UWC was successful, and it could not have happened at a better time. A year earlier, Professor Jakes Gerwel, soon to be rector of UWC, had issued a clarion call: 'The University of the Western Cape is open to all and is the home of the democratic left intellectual.' It felt as if Gerwel had an eager, young, wannabe intellectual like me in mind.

My mother couldn't contain her emotions when I broke the news. 'Hallelujah! Congratulations!' she exclaimed. 'I'm glad you didn't give up.' She hugged me, wiping away a tear. It was a major milestone for the Abrahams family and unprecedented in Nooitgedacht. The few who made it to college or university mostly ended up studying teaching. My decision broke with that tradition. We relished the moment, but none of us dared raise the subject of tuition fees.

In the weeks leading to the start of the academic year, I asked a few people to assist me with the cost of textbooks, which I needed immediately, and decided to leave tuition fees for later. Father Henry was one of my intended textbook benefactors. He was the Catholic priest in Bishop Lavis, and known as the poor man's priest. Father Henry had devoted many years of his life to serving the poor and the sick in and around our neighbourhoods. To most locals, he was a hero. To the apartheid government, he was a thorn in the flesh. When not at the pulpit, he was out marching alongside pepper-sprayed protestors, calling for an end to the injustice of apartheid.

He reminded me of Father Gabriel from the 1986 movie *The Mission*, a Jesuit priest who lives in the South American jungle among the indigenous Guarani people, whom he converts to Christianity. He also converts Rodrigo Mendoza, a former slave trader, and convinces him to become a priest as penance for the evils he has committed against the Guarani. When Father Gabriel learns that Portuguese colonialists seek to enslave the Guarani, and that the papal emissary has decided to close the mission station, he sides with the Guarani. Mendoza takes up arms against the Portuguese and is killed, but Gabriel opts for non-violence. This was the spirit Father Henry epitomised.

After I revealed the purpose of my visit, Father Henry offered his congratulations and sat me down to explain the importance of education and its service to the community. 'Law should be in service of the public and not just the self,' he counselled me. Then, like a good father, he made me kneel down and blessed me with a little prayer. Afterwards, he disappeared into his office only to return, smiling, with a fifty-rand note in his hand. 'May God bless you,' he said, handing it to me. As I walked out of his presbytery, I made a promise to heed his advice. Father Henry's money and another R150 I collected bought me most of my textbooks for the first term.

UWC lived up to my expectations as a home of the democratic left intellectual, and I loved the hip vibe. Some students went about their normal academic routines, while in the cafeteria and student hall others were busy with political debates. UWC even threw up a few surprises. Cassiem Christians, who I hadn't seen since our detention in Victor Verster, had enrolled as a first-year student in the Arts Faculty. We were thrilled to see each other and rekindled our old camaraderie.

University life, however, was demanding, and my ignorance of the law was patently obvious. In one assignment, I was asked to provide legal reasons why the minister of home affairs acted unlawfully when, in November 1986, he confiscated the passport of anti-apartheid cleric Dr Allan Boesak. This occurred on the eve of Boesak's intended visit to the United States, where he was due to receive a human rights award from the Robert F. Kennedy Memorial. My intuitive response was that it was political spitefulness. The correct answer was that, in legal terms, it was irrational, unlawful and unreasonable. Even though this was only my first year, my mind was a long way from being moulded into thinking like a lawyer.

Meanwhile, Cassiem was spending most of his time in the cafeteria, engaged in student politics. It worried me, but he was unperturbed about his studies. 'Politics runs deep in my veins,' he reminded me whenever I rebuked him for not attending classes. I attended classes religiously, but student politics engaged me too and I frequently went to political talks. One such was a lunchtime talk by AZAPO on the prevailing political situation in the country. I was interested in AZAPO, whose roots were anchored in Steve Biko's Black Consciousness Movement.

The lecture room was full, with students standing in the aisles, but the atmosphere was relaxed. I was seated next to Cassiem, towards the middle. The talk had hardly begun when a group of chanting students forced their way into the room. From the freedom songs they sang, I thought they'd come to join the lecture, but when I heard 'Out, you bastards! Out!' I knew we were in trouble. The atmosphere changed to panic as students fled in all directions. Petrified, I immediately tried to leave.

'Where are you going?' Cassiem snapped, pulling me down. He stood up and berated the fleeing students. 'Stop! Come back and sit down!' The chanting students then turned and came towards us. I was terrified, but when Cassiem calmly took off his jacket, the group suddenly stopped in their tracks and made an abrupt about-turn. Only then did I see the bulging silver firearm on his right hip. It sent shivers down my spine. My mind immediately flashed back to my time in detention when a fellow detainee had warned me about Cassiem – that he was a radical Muslim who'd shot at police when they'd entered a mosque.

The group hurried out of the lecture room. Cassiem and I followed and found a tense stand-off ensuing outside. I watched in disbelief as AZAPO students faced down students of the ANC-aligned United Democratic Front (UDF). I'd witnessed many horrible stand-offs between rival gangs, but never a political stand-off. It was a surreal experience at the home of the democratic left intellectual. Eventually, campus security intervened and dispersed us all. The incident had exposed the fragile foundations upon which Professor Gerwel's idea was built: there was nothing democratic or intellectual about fights between these leftists.

Afterwards, I learnt that the confrontation stemmed from an age-old ideological battle that went back to the days of the Russian Revolution and the ideological differences between Joseph Stalin and Leon Trotsky. Those differences had resulted in Trotsky's untimely death in 1940, at the hands of one of Stalin's assassins. According to some leftists, this cursed ideological battle apparently found its way into South African liberation politics between the so-called ANC 'Stalinists' and AZAPO 'Trotskyites'. Whether this feud had any substance or not, it was my first taste of the bitterness in UWC politics, and it wasn't the last.

As the academic year drew to a close, I could no longer ignore the issue of my unpaid tuition fees; the university wanted its pound of flesh. My problems were further compounded by my results, which were a mixed bag: I passed some subjects, failed others. With weak results and outstanding fees, I faced the dire prospect of academic exclusion the following year. Caught in a tailspin, I asked Cassiem for help. He managed to strong-arm a few rands out of his friends, but it wasn't enough to clear my debts. As a last resort, I appealed to Uncle Lennie, a local Presbyterian minister.

I'd known Uncle Lennie since my childhood on the outskirts of Elsies River. He too had moved to Nooitgedacht with his family. He knew some people at the university and, without hesitation, agreed to help. About a week later, he came back to me.

'I've got good news for you,' he said, all excited. 'I've secured a place for you.'

I'd known he could pull it off, and thanked him profusely. 'You're a lifesaver, Uncle Lennie.'

But there was a punchline to the good news. 'Charles,' he said, pausing for a moment, 'I could only secure you a place at the Theology Faculty.'

My excitement instantly waned. 'Theology! Why theology?'

Uncle Lennie simply smiled. 'Yes! Theology.'

I was gutted by the news. I'd had my fair share of religion and had no appetite for more. But there was not much choice. Desperate to study, I accepted the offer.

I tried to make the best of a reluctant year of religious studies by gaining greater insight into Christian beliefs. The course on the New Testament depicted God as a loving God, different from the vengeful, biased and jealous Old Testament God I'd encountered during my time in the Cape Town library. John 3:16 says, 'For God so loved the world, that He gave his only Son, that whoever believes in Him should not perish but have eternal life.' I realised that the God of my birth and upbringing may very well have been two different Gods or one with multiple personalities. Perhaps that explained the contradictions in my father's behaviour towards my mother.

What perplexed me even further was the belief in the Holy Trinity – the idea of God the Father, God the Son and God the Holy Ghost as one and the same God. Perhaps there was something deeper here that I couldn't grasp, but even so, it boggled my mind that, centuries earlier, church fathers had simply adopted the concept of the Holy Trinity by a majority show of hands, resulting in a major schism between Trinitarians and non-Trinitarians, the latter being branded as heretics and outcasts.

When the year ended, I couldn't wait to get back into law. My father, who had decided to support my endeavour to study further, settled my student debts with a loan from work. My mother undertook to pay my fees out of the household food budget. All I needed to do was convince the university that I could pay my tuition.

I managed to schedule a meeting with the university's head of finance. After waiting for almost an hour outside his office, I was allowed in. The bespectacled official was deeply immersed in work and hardly acknowledged me when I sat down. I might as well have spoken to a brick wall, because he showed no interest as I pleaded my case.

'It's clear you can't afford to be at this university,' he said when he eventually raised his head. 'I can't let you continue.'

I stared in disbelief. 'I promise I'll pay my tuition fees. Just let me study!' I begged, but he was unmoved and resumed his work.

I walked out of his office in tears. My legs wobbled as I made my way through the student centre, clutching my small backpack. Music blasted in the background, while students played klawerjas. I shot them a dirty look. All I wanted to do was study law and there they were, playing stupid card games. I dragged myself to the train station, feeling worse than I ever had in my life. I just wanted to sulk by myself.

I sat down in a corner of a quiet carriage. The home of the democratic left intellectual had led me right back to where I'd started, and my hopes of becoming a lawyer seemed to be in tatters.

Two young men stared at me, probably taking pity on me. I ignored them. But as the train moved out of the station, they got up and walked in my direction. I thought they were changing carriages, but when they sat next to me, I realised something was wrong. One took out a knife and threatened me. The other demanded my watch.

Why this too, dear Lord? I cried to myself as I looked at them. Already down and out, I had nothing to lose. So I lost my shit. Profanities rolled from my tongue like never before: 'Julle ma se poese! Julle fokken naaiers! Los my fokken uit!' I yelled. (Your mothers' cunts! You fucking fuckers! Leave me the fuck alone!) I don't know how many times I yelled at them, adding, 'En UWC se ma se poes!' for good measure.

Shocked, the men backed off and quickly left the carriage at the next stop. I don't know whether they fled because they thought I was deranged or I'd attracted too much attention to the attempted robbery. An elderly woman with a young child came over to console me.

'Come sit here by us,' she said in a gentle voice as she took me by the hand.

I started to cry again as I followed her to her seat. 'All I wanted to do was to study.'

'Don't worry, everything will be fine,' she comforted me.

By the time the train got to Bishop Lavis station, I'd composed myself and thanked her.

—m—

My parents had been expecting the bad news; they knew I would have difficulty finishing university without financial support. Surprisingly, neither of them pressured me into finding a job. Even though I had no clear idea of what to do next, I did not want to give up on studying law. While figuring out how I could get back to university, I decided to put my one year of legal studies to good use and started a free, informal legal-advice office from my parents' home. It was an instant hit with the locals. The demand was so overwhelming that it became a full-time affair.

Other than the problem of gang violence, the plight of single mothers was appalling. They received hardly any child support from absent or imprisoned fathers, and were left to fend, often unemployed, for themselves and their children. With the support of a few parents, I started an informal day-care centre in Bream Way. Uncle Jonny and Aunty Gurtie from down the road readily agreed to make their back-yard shack available.

Not everyone liked the idea. The local municipality threatened to close the facility, as it did not comply with municipal regulations. Local 'verkrampte' (reactionary) politicians who'd cooperated with the apartheid government called for its closure, claiming it was a front for ANC terrorists, all because I'd served time in detention. But the community vowed to resist any attempts to close the crèche. Even the Josters and the Flat Boys, whose members had children at the crèche, came out in support: 'Nai, my bru! Moenie worry nie. Laat die naaiers net fokken probeer die crèche toemaak, dan sal hulle sien. Ons sal hulle in hulle poes skiet.' (No, my brother! Don't worry. Let those fuckers just try to close the crèche and then they'll see. We'll fucking shoot them.) It was proof that even gangsters wanted what was good for their children. If only they could have used that same vigour for the good of the whole community.

In time, I teamed up with Mrs Stevens – a retired teacher from Bishop Lavis – and two others (Mrs Benny and Mr Claasen), to set up adult literacy classes in Bishop Lavis and Valhalla Park. Young and old joined to learn to read and write. The most popular of my endeavours was a weekly soup kitchen I set up with the help of Kevin Kiewitz and Kelvin Vollenhoven, two university mates with whom I'd kept contact. They proved to be true friends and comrades: once a week, they'd fill

Kevin's ragged Volkswagen Golf with pots of soup made by volunteer mothers and head for Nooitgedacht. It was an opportunity to bring kids from Bream Way and the flats together in weekly fun and games, away from their mock gang fights, and the kids thoroughly enjoyed it.

With only a year of law and theology behind me, I was a barefoot lawyer, counsellor and even a lay minister to some. I earned a small monthly stipend from small-donor benefactors, and this allowed me to resume my law studies in 1991. I returned to UWC, and for the next four years I devoted myself to studying part-time. It was a time of zealous juggling, where I worked during the day and attended classes at night, but it paid off in joy when I completed my B.Proc degree in 1994. The moment called for celebration but, given my earlier exclusion, I opted to skip my graduation ceremony.

14

A brave new world

It's amazing how one's fortunes can change overnight. With a law degree to my name, I was no longer on the bottom rung – I'd moved up a couple of notches. My timing couldn't have been better; I'd finished my degree the same year that South Africa held its first free and democratic elections. There were two places in South Africa where budding lawyers wanted to be: the Constitutional Court and the Legal Resources Centre (LRC), South Africa's prestigious public interest law centre. I'd been accepted to do my two-year articles of clerkship at the LRC. By then, I was already twenty-eight, older than most law clerks.

The demise of apartheid brought about a constitutional democracy, or what some described as a constitutional juristocracy, a system where the constitution is king. The LRC teemed with lawyers and in its corridors you could bump into George Bizos (who defended Nelson Mandela at the Rivonia Trial), Arthur Chaskalson (a founding member of the LRC and newly appointed president of the Constitutional Court) and many more. It was a heady time, especially as the first Constitutional Court cases were brought by the LRC. One of those concerned the death penalty. In a matter of months, the Constitutional Court declared section 277 of the Criminal Procedure Act – which prescribed the death penalty as a competent sentence for murder – inconsistent with the constitution and invalid. In another LRC case, the court declared it unconstitutional to imprison those who were unable to pay their debts, marking a welcome relief for the poor and indigent.

I did not work on any landmark cases, but I had my hands full with everyday cases of unlawful evictions, police shootings and unfair dismissals of mostly indigent clients. I soon learnt that case preparation and procedure were as important as the substance of cases. From early on, my supervisor, Steve Kahanovitz, had me on a leash, drilling into me the basics of proper note-taking and meticulous case preparation. But despite the invaluable experience that Steve and the LRC provided, I was on a mission to make up for lost time and finish my articles of clerkship in one year rather than the usual two, so I could establish my own practice sooner rather than later.

To do so, there were a few hurdles it was necessary to jump. First, I had to undertake practical legal training at the University of Cape Town's School for Legal Practice. That would reduce my articles to one year. It also meant starting my daily routine at five in the morning to prepare for work, which finished at five in the afternoon. Then it was off to UCT. Classes finished at nine and I would be home by ten. Next, I had to pass four attorneys' admission examinations at the same time. This meant sacrificing my weekends. It was a huge gamble, but the effort paid off. I completed the university course, passed all my admission examinations and shortened my articles by a year. On 2 February 1996, I was admitted as an attorney of the Western Cape High Court.

To many, the news came as a surprise, and I was thrust into the spotlight: a hero of Nooitgedacht. Locals came in their droves to congratulate me, even those from the former 'white' side of Nooitgedacht. The demise of apartheid had unceremoniously eroded the superiority of their white-coloured world and, in time, many of them became my loyal clients. I didn't make much of my newfound status, however; I knew that more hard work awaited me.

I'd decided to open up my practice at my parents' house despite my colleagues cautioning against it. 'Professional suicide,' some warned. 'You will never make it.' Unfortunately, I had little choice; my bank refused to provide me with a loan to kick-start the practice because I was deemed a high credit risk, and I couldn't afford to rent an office. With no money, I feared my colleagues' warnings would come true.

Unlike many young start-up practices, however, my client base had been long in the making. Many of the Flat Boys and Josters were my primary- and high-school mates who'd dropped out of school. They'd since been absorbed into the much feared 26s and 28s Numbers gangs.

Locals referred to them as 'die sesse' (the sixes) and 'die agge' (the eights), and their turf war had become a deadly drug war. With no shortage of crime – drug dealing, possession of unlicensed firearms, murder, robbery, assault and rape – there was plenty of work.

I knew this situation would present me with many moral dilemmas, and my would-be clients were already regarded as the scum of the earth. To me, however, they were simply my clients. I saw no reason to turn my back on them, more so because I had grown up with and lived among them. I decided to deal with ethics on a case-by-case basis. With only a small desk and cupboard, a knock-up filing cabinet and a second-hand typewriter, I got to work.

—ww—

My practice brought a sense of respectability to our home. My mother was grateful that one of her children had made a success of their life. Even my father boasted about my achievements, much to my annoyance, given his initial ambivalence towards my studies. As for the rest of my family, Mara had married and moved in with her husband in the nearby vaal flats. Francois, who'd long since left the house and joined the PAC in exile in Zimbabwe, had returned to South Africa and was now living in Johannesburg. He occasionally visited the family home. Roseline, Marius and Anneline did well at high school, but not so Christopher and Johan. Johan was dyslexic and had dropped out of school. He did occasional work as a mechanic, but spent most of his time hanging out with fellow drop-outs on the street corner. For Christopher, the temptation of alcohol was too great. He failed Standard 9 and dropped out of school.

Amanda and Ronel had blossomed into beautiful teenagers, but both had a mean streak that caused my mother additional grief with their unprovoked rage. I took a personal interest in the well-being of Lorenzo, my youngest brother, and Mara's first-born son, Montesquieu, and sought to protect them from the social ills of our neighbourhood.

Finally, love beckoned. Mean-spirited Sasman and his family had moved out of Nooitgedacht and sold their house to Merilyn, a single mother from Elsies River. Her lively spirit was a breath of fresh air in Bream Way. She was ten years older than me, but looked much younger than her age. She knocked me off my feet, and I was so head over heels for this vivacious woman that it didn't take long for a relationship to develop. Months later, I moved in with her and her five-year-old son, Marco. Life was on the up and I thought it could only get better.

15

A not so brave new world

It was a perfect afternoon. The glowing February sun sat at its zenith, and the dogs lazed around the house. I'd finished court early and returned to the office at my parents' house. When I pulled up in the shabby Alfa Romeo I'd bought two years before, I saw a car parked outside the gate, and before I could settle down there was a knock on the door. 'Come inside,' I called out. A wrinkled woman entered. She wore a big pair of round, 1980s-style glasses. I guessed she was in her late sixties.

'Middag, meneer. Mag ek maar inkom? Ek het vir u gewag,' she said in a soft, shaky voice. (Good day, sir. May I come in? I've been waiting for you.) She introduced herself as Mrs Bessant.

'What brings you here?' I asked.

'I read about your success in the newspaper. Congratulations, Mr Abrahams.' Then she got straight to the purpose of her visit. 'I've come to see you about my baby boy, Wayne. He was taken into custody two days ago for kidnapping and rape.'

I interrupted her to get my notepad, and that's when I noticed my seventeen-year-old sister Amanda walking briskly up and down outside in her pink nightgown. My mouth went dry.

About a year or so earlier, Amanda had been diagnosed with schizophrenia and had since been in and out of mental hospitals. Her psychosis had gone from bad to worse. My heart plummeted at the sight of her distress, but I didn't know what to do. Mrs Bessant sat quietly in the corner, consumed by her son's troubles, unaware of the trouble brewing outside. Unsure how to proceed, I went back to my desk and took notes, hoping that Amanda would calm down and come back inside.

'My son is accused of being part of a group of men who abducted a fifteen-year-old girl and gang-raped her,' Mrs Bessant told me. 'But he couldn't have done it. I know that for sure, 'cause my baby would never hurt a fly. I want you to get him out of custody and prove that he is innocent. Please, Mr Abrahams,' she begged, desperate.

I could barely concentrate with Amanda on my mind. When I eventually looked out the window, my worst fears were confirmed: Amanda was having a psychotic breakdown. She was lying on the ground and had covered herself, head to toe, with sand. My legs trembled. Mrs Bessant could see something was wrong.

'Are you okay, Mr Abrahams?"

I nodded, fully aware that I had to act quickly. 'I'm sorry Mrs Bessant, but I must attend to something urgently,' I said. 'Do you mind coming back tomorrow?'

She hesitantly agreed and left the office, walking directly to where Amanda lay. She stopped, looked at Amanda and me with pity, and carried on. I was deeply embarrassed, but also concerned about Amanda. I tried to keep calm.

With Mrs Bessant out of the way, I went into overdrive. When Amanda lapsed into delusional states, she heard the voices of people wanting to kill her and became aggressive, so I was concerned that she'd turn violent. By the time I reached her, my mother and Rosaline were already outside, urging her to get up. I joined them, grabbing Amanda by the arms. Her arms were stiff and her hands were balled into fists. I knew she was preparing for a fight.

'We have to get her to Valkenberg as quick as possible,' I yelled at my mother and Roseline. Valkenberg was a psychiatric hospital in Observatory, about fifteen kilometres away. Mara came to assist us. My mother must have called her.

As we lifted Amanda from the ground, she began to shout, 'You! You! You want to kill me! I know you're after me!'

Staying resolute and focused, we bundled her into my car.

'Don't take me to that fucking mad place!' Amanda screamed. 'I don't want to go there!' She threw wild punches at her sisters, who were desperately trying to restrain her. I reversed out of the driveway, blows raining on my head.

'Everything will be okay, Amanda,' I tried to persuade her.

'Fuck you! Fuck you! It's not okay. Let me out of this fucking car,' she howled. 'I don't want to go to that fucking mad hospital. It's the doctors there that make me mad.'

Mara and Roseline tightened their grip on her and made sure the rear doors were locked so that she couldn't jump out. As I drove, I ducked a few more blows whenever she managed to break free. Near the hospital, Amanda ground her teeth and stiffened her body as she tried to pull free. She was like a raging cow that had smelt death beyond the gates of an abattoir. When we drove onto the hospital's premises, she broke loose and started punching me.

'Jou vark! Jou vark! Ek hoort nie in die mal plek nie,' she yelled. (You pig! You pig! I don't belong in this mad place.)

With one hand on the steering wheel and another shielding the blows, I made it to the admissions ward. It took the three of us and a male nurse to get Amanda out of the car and into the ward, where the nurses immediately sedated her. We were exhausted, but breathed a sigh of relief. Several hours later, the psychiatrist assessed her and decided to keep her at the hospital.

No one spoke on our way home. Roseline and Mara looked embarrassed and apologised to me.

'No need to apologise,' I said, realising that I should never have opened my practice at home.

After all that drama, I was surprised to see Mrs Bessant back at the office the following day.

'Is the young lady okay?' she enquired.

'Yes,' I responded, too ashamed to go into detail. I'd already decided to take on her son's case, as I felt compassion for the old lady. I made the necessary preparations to see him at court.

'You're a good person,' she said when she thanked me, visibly relieved.

I met Wayne in the holding cells on the day of his court appearance. He was scruffy, unshaven and smelt unwashed. Mrs Bessant was right about the demeanour of her 'baby boy'. Wayne was soft-spoken, slim and certainly passive. After I'd introduced myself, we sat down and he told his story.

Wayne had been driving to visit a friend in Parkwood Estate, but had got lost. He asked three guys for directions, and they offered to drive with him and show him the way. Once they were in the car, however, it became obvious that they had no idea where the friend lived. Nevertheless, they insisted that Wayne buy them beers in return for their efforts.

Before going to a smokkie for the beers, Wayne stopped at a garage for petrol. One of the guys, Jimmy, got out of the car to talk to a group of girls, and tried to force one of them to come with him to the car. She resisted and ran away, but Jimmy jumped back into Wayne's car and ordered him to drive after the girl, yelling, 'Djy! Jou poes! Ry jou naai! Ry agter dai goose aan!' (You! You cunt! Drive, you fuck! Drive after that girl!)

Shaking, Wayne started the car and drove after the running girl, with another of the guys, Tony, yelling, 'Ry! Jou naai! Ry vinnag!' (Drive! You fuck! Drive faster!) When they got close, the girl ran on to the property of a house, but Jimmy jumped out and dragged her, screaming, into the car. The third guy, Joey, shouted at Wayne, 'Ry, jou tief! Ry! Voor ek jou met die mes vrek stiek.' (Drive, you bitch! Drive! Before I kill you with this knife.)

Wayne was told to drive to the Wynberg Fire Station, where Jimmy and Tony dragged the girl from the car to the back of the station.

'She was screaming and pleading with them not to hurt her,' Wayne told me. 'She was just a child, Mr Abrahams.'

After waiting at the car for a few minutes, Joey forced Wayne, at knifepoint, to follow the others to the back of the station. There, Tony was kicking and slapping the girl where she lay on the ground, begging him to stop. Jimmy pointed a gun at Wayne and ordered him to hold her legs. When he obeyed, Tony took hold of her arms and Joey shut her mouth. Jimmy pulled down her jeans and panties, then unbuckled his belt, pulled down his own pants and penetrated her. She was unable to scream, but Wayne could see the pain on her face, and he began to sob as he recounted the story to me.

'Hy was soes 'n fokken hond, Mr Abrahams, die manier hoe hy ha' gerape het, aan en aan en aan.' (He was like a fucking dog, Mr Abrahams, the way he raped her, on and on and on.)

All three men raped the girl. When they had finished, she was silent and her legs were spattered with blood. 'Your turn!' Jimmy said to Wayne, pointing the gun at him and ordering him to pull down his pants. Again, Wayne obeyed, but when he couldn't get an erection the men laughed and told him to pull his pants back up. They bundled the girl into the car and Wayne drove back to Parkwood Estate. Along the way, they kicked the girl out of the car as if disposing of a used condom.

Wayne was made to go to Tony's house with him, presumably to prevent him from going straight to the police. Nevertheless, the police came to the house later that night and arrested them both. The girl must have known the three men and reported their crimes. Jimmy was arrested too, but Joey disappeared.

The barbarity of Wayne's story was so abhorrent that I couldn't maintain my professional composure. 'Fucking bastards,' I kept mumbling. But I believed in Wayne's honesty and was convinced he should get bail. Which was what happened. Mrs Bessant was tearfully relieved.

The next step was to get the charges against him withdrawn. I approached the prosecutor and advised her that Wayne was prepared to turn state witness and provide testimony against the other accused. The prosecutor agreed. At the court hearing a few months later, the testimonies delivered by both Wayne and the young woman were sufficient to convince the magistrate that the hoodlums each deserved a sentence of fourteen years.

Wayne and his mother couldn't thank me enough. 'Die Here gaan jou nog vele male seën,' Mrs Bessant said, hugging me. (God will still bless you many more times.) I was pleased that his case had had a happy ending, but it left me appalled. For years I'd seen, first-hand, the brutal violence against women on the Cape Flats, yet I couldn't come to terms with the savagery of those three young rapists. Whatever their socio-economic circumstances, I could find no justification for their barbarism. The professional, political and moral tensions within me were brought to the fore, and it was only the first of many such cases that would pull me into often competing directions.

16

Ketie's son

Amanda's psychotic breakdown had disturbed the uneasy peace at home, and soon after, I confronted another reason why I should not have set up my practice at my parents' house. One afternoon, I discovered that my safe, with all my clients' money, had been emptied out. After a quick inquiry, I suspected my brother Johan. Roseline confirmed my suspicion when she told me he'd been hanging about my office in the morning and then disappeared. Livid, I drove to his local drinking hole in the vaal flats, cursing him profusely.

As I pulled up, teenagers hanging around outside the smokkie hastily made way. The owner told me that Johan had been there earlier but had left. I drove around the neighbourhood on the off-chance that I might spot him. I met with no success, and went home to wait for him.

Johan walked into the lounge late that night, reeking of alcohol and dagga.

'Where's my money?' I demanded.

'What money?' he said. 'What do you mean? I didn't steal your money.'

I'd reached boiling point. I punched him in the face and he stumbled.

'Stop, stop!' my mother yelled.

But I didn't. I kept on hitting him until Roseline pulled me away. Johan's face was covered in blood, and my knuckles were bloody and bruised. He got to his feet and staggered out of the house, swearing at me. My mother sobbed while Roseline shook her head in disbelief. Distraught, I too left the house and drove off into the night.

The next morning, I found my mother in the lounge, exhausted. After I'd left, my father had argued with her about the theft of the money. He was angry that I'd hit Johan and had lambasted her for not intervening, leaving her emotionally drained. I dropped down next to her. Now was the time to talk about my father, and I did not want to let the moment pass. Even though her voice was weary, it seemed she'd been waiting for this opportunity.

'Ek wou lankal julle pa laat los het, maar ek moes dink aan julle,' she said. (I would have left your father long ago, but I had to think of all of you.) After their marriage, my mother learnt that he was having an affair with another woman and had conceived a child with her. She was devastated. When she confronted him, he denied it. Later he confessed, but became angry and hit her. My mother fled the house with Mara and went to stay with a friend.

'Van daai tyd af is ek bang vir jou pa. Jy weet dit en het dit self gesien.' (From that time on, I've been afraid of your father. You know it and have seen it for yourself.) She paused, tears flowing.

Mara was not my father's daughter; my mother had fallen pregnant with her in an earlier relationship. Her parents had not approved, and had accused her of bringing shame to the family. 'Ek en Mara het swaar gekry,' she said. 'Ek het besluit om haar te vernoem na die bybelse Mara wat ook swaar gekry het.' (Mara and I had a difficult experience. I decided to name her after the biblical Mara, who also had a difficult life.) I listened quietly.

Rather than stay with her family, my mother left their home in Aberdeen and came to Cape Town. She didn't know a soul in the city, except for a very distant friend who offered them temporary accommodation. For a while they moved from place to place, scurrying like stray dogs. Those were hard days, and my mother's only income was from odd cleaning jobs. Then she met my father at church. He came across as a good man and the congregants spoke highly of him. She found it funny that they called him Broer Baard even though he was bald and had no beard. Despite her tears, she smiled as she recalled these memories. It didn't take them long to start seeing each other, fall in love and get married. It was a wonderful time of her life.

The one drawback was that my father could never pronounce her name properly, because he had no front teeth. Instead of saying

Kathleen, he said 'Ketleen'. To make it easier for him, my mother let him call her Kathy, but that was a mistake because he ended up calling her 'Ketie'. Nevertheless, she took pity on him and allowed him to call her Ketie as long as she could tease him now and then by calling him Broer Baard.

There was a little laughter in her voice as she told me this, but it was short-lived. After the bliss of getting married, his affair came as a hard blow, and things were never the same. When I asked her why she did not leave my father, she said it wasn't that easy: she and Mara had nowhere to go. So she endured, hoping their situation would get better, but it didn't.

We were both quiet for a moment. Then I asked the question that had long puzzled me: 'But why so many children, Mommy?'

She looked at me as if I'd offended her and turned her face away. After a while, she responded. 'You will not understand how hard it is for a woman with no power.' She turned towards me. 'What do you do when your whole life is so dependent on a man who expects everything of you, your entire body and soul? There were so many things I wanted to do, but I put them aside for the sake of you children.' Concealing her emotions, she looked at me and said, 'But you have made me proud. I'm so happy with your achievements.'

I hugged her tightly, but felt awful. I wished I could take her burdens off her shoulders. 'I should be the one proud of you for raising me,' I said. As I walked out of the lounge, I felt honoured to be Ketie's son. More than ever, I was determined to make a success of my practice and make her even more proud.

17

Die Nek
(The Neck)

Colin Stanfield. No other name evoked as much fear and terror on the Cape Flats. It's said that few people dared cross his path for fear of death. Some likened him to Al Capone, the notorious mobster who headed the Chicago Outfit in the 1930s, but to those within his inner circle he was known as 'Die Nek' (The Neck), a name synonymous with the Mafia title 'The Don'. Colin was the boss of all bosses.

I had no reason to believe our paths would cross, but one evening, my brother Marius informed me that Stanfield wanted to see me. Marius had been a golf caddy when he met Stanfield and since then the two had become regular golfing buddies. Despite my initial apprehension, Marius persuaded me to meet this man whose life was shrouded in mystery. It was said he'd started as a humble fruit and vegetable vendor, and had rapidly expanded his business across the Cape Flats until apartheid restrictions drove it into the ground. He'd remained underground ever since. One story had it that he turned to bootlegging, setting up smokkelhuise (illegal shebeens) selling alcohol, but was quickly put out of business. Tired of the stumbling blocks, he decided to grow the largest drug trade on the Cape Flats.

Whatever the truth, it was his association with the notorious 28s gang that had tongues wagging. Apparently, he was its undeclared leader, and he combined his vast underworld enterprise with the 28s to form the feared criminal enterprise known as The Firm. Despite the allegations surrounding Stanfield, most of the locals in his neighbourhood regarded him as a hero. Each year, thousands of people lined up for his end-of-year Christmas party in Valhalla Park, where he personally doled out hundreds of thousands of rands. This was his way of giving back to the community.

Marius told me our meeting was fixed for the following day. 'Go to the purple double-storey house in Hazel Street in Valhalla Park,' he instructed me. 'You won't miss it; it's the only house of its kind in Valhalla Park. You'll find him there. He's tall, a bit burly and has a scar on the right of his face.'

The next day, I went straight from court to Valhalla Park. In Hazel Street, a group of young men stood beside a brand-new yellow BMW M3 parked in front of a purple house. Mindful of my old green Alfa Romeo, I parked a few metres away. Everyone's eyes were fixed on me as I got out. I felt out of place in my suit. No one said a word as I approached.

'Is Mr Colin Stanfield here?' I asked nervously.

'Who are you?' one of the young men asked from behind dark Ray-Bans.

'I'm a lawyer. Mr Stanfield asked to see me.'

The group stared at me and at my car as if to say, What kind of shit lawyer drives a battered car like that? They pointed me to the house.

At the door, I was greeted by the aromatic smell of fried meat and a woman who introduced herself as Jenny. 'Come inside,' she said, ushering me into the lounge. 'Colin!' she called. 'Die lawyer is hie.' (The lawyer is here.)

Colin sat alone on a huge brown leather couch in a smoky corner. But for the distinctive scar on his face, I would not have recognised him. He put out his cigarette and got up to greet me.

'Middag, meneer Abrahams. Dankie dat u my kô' siennit.' (Good day, Mr Abrahams. Thank you for coming to see me.)

He smiled. His four front teeth were absent. His respectful manner surprised me, and I greeted him formally as Mr Stanfield. He insisted I call him by his first name. Then he shouted, 'Jenny! Bring koffie.' She dutifully obliged.

'Congratulations on your success,' he said. 'I'm very glad to hear that someone from our own community has done so well as to qualify as a lawyer.' Then he got straight to the point. 'Over many years, I've given a lot of my business to white lawyers. Now that we've got someone from our own community, I would like to give you some of my work.' He slurped coffee from a saucer. 'What type of work does Mr Abrahams do?'

'All kinds of work, Mr Stanfield. Sorry, Colin.' I grinned nervously.

'Good,' he said. 'From now on, I will pass on most of my work to you.' I hadn't expected our meeting to result in work from him. Too surprised, I didn't enquire about the kind of work.

Our conversation switched to golf. How I managed an hour-long discussion about the sport still defeats me. By the time I left, the group of young men had warmed up to me: 'Goodbye, Mr Lawyer.'

—⁂—

Over the next few months, I experienced an unprecedented surge in criminal work from Stanfield, and my telephone rang incessantly.

'Dis Bal, meneer. Ek stuur nog 'n saak vir meneer.' (It's Bal, sir. I'm sending another case for you, sir.) Bal was Stanfield's right-hand man. My workload grew so quickly that I commanded cases in courts all over Cape Town – Bishop Lavis, Goodwood, Bellville, the city centre, Wynberg and Mitchells Plain. Prosecutors and magistrates got to know me. Some of my colleagues quietly referred to me as The Firm's lawyer, a label I detested. Overnight, I was thrust into a surreal world of defending some of the Cape Flats' most hardened street and prison gangsters. Even though I'd spent most of my life growing up around gang culture, I'd never had a glimpse of their inner world. Defending gang members gave me some insight.

It's said that the worlds of street and prison gangs were never meant to mix; each was supposed to have maintained their separate dominions. These strictures dated back more than a century, to the world of Nongoloza and Kilikijan, the former a young Zulu and the latter a young Pondo. The two were incensed by the injustices they'd personally experienced under British colonial rule. In 1886, nineteen-year-old

Nongoloza, whose real name was Mzuzepi Mathebula (alias Note), was working as a groom for his white master, Mr Tom. One of Mr Tom's horses went missing while grazing in the field, on a day when Nongoloza had been assigned to garden duties. Mr Tom threatened to have the young Nongoloza jailed if he did not find the horse or pay back its value, equivalent to two years of his wages. Nongoloza was so incensed at the injustice that he left Mr Tom's employ and headed for Johannesburg. There he met Kilikijan and the two resorted to a life of crime that ultimately led to their imprisonment.

Nongoloza and a group of eight men became known as the 28s, the fighting ones who worked by night. Kilikijan had seven men and they became the 27s, the ones who worked during the day. The number 2 presumably represented the two men. When they landed in jail, they met six men who gambled, smuggled and accrued wealth, and these men became known as the 26s. Thus, the Numbers world was born. It was only meant for prison, but Nongoloza and Kilikijan's hierarchies found their way out of prison and intertwined with street gangs, forming a toxic mix. Nowhere were its lethal consequences more evident than on the Cape Flats. Take, for example, the case of Waheed 'Mafylan' Adams of Kensington.

Mafylan was a 28 charged with the murder of a rival 26 gang member. He was being held at Pollsmoor Prison and my instructions were to get him out on bail. I'd represented many baby-faced young men, and Mafylan was no exception. He was tall and slender, probably in his early twenties. He wasted no time getting down to business.

'Mr Abrahams, can you get me out of here?' He stared, unblinking, at me. Experience suggested he was testing to see how tough I was: if I couldn't get him out, I was wasting his time. I had to remain strong.

'What crime do the police say you've committed?' I asked, deflecting his question.

It got him talking. 'They say I'm a Kasba gang member and a hitman for the 28s. They say that in a house in Lost City in Mitchells Plain I shot dead Gary, a 26 of the Bad Boys gang.'

'What do you say about it?'

'Nie, meneer!' he protested. 'Dit wassie ekkie. Daai tyd was ek by die huis. Ek het TV gekyk.' (No, sir! It wasn't me. That time I was at home. I was watching TV.)

I asked more questions and answers followed. I took copious notes. By the time I got the police docket, Mafylan's story wasn't as simple. At the time of his death, Gary's girlfriend was at the house and had identified Mafylan, even though the man she saw had been wearing a mask. From her testimony, it appeared that four men had burst into the house, found Gary sleeping in the bedroom with his two-year-old son and pumped nine bullets into his body at close range, miraculously missing the little boy. 'When I got into the room after they'd left,' the girlfriend had testified, 'blood oozed out of his head and body. I shouted, "My baby! My baby!"'

Despite the grisly details, the state's case wasn't as strong as it looked. Gary's girlfriend couldn't positively identify Mafylan other than saying that the person looked and laughed like him. Also, she had no idea who fired the fatal shots. Given these uncertainties, the magistrate granted Mafylan bail.

Unlike the case with Wayne, son of elderly Mrs Bessant, I wasn't excited about Mafylan's case. I was distraught by how audacious gang life on the Cape Flats had become. It made the street fights between the Josters and Flat Boys look like amateur skirmishes.

My next case was Alan 'Donnie' Daniels, also charged with murder. He too was being held at Pollsmoor and, like Mafylan, was accused of being a hitman for the 28s. Donnie had allegedly entered a house in Valhalla Park and shot a rival 26 in cold blood. His case was ready for trial. It was my first murder trial and I was nervous. Despite weeks of preparation, I stumbled and failed to properly cross-examine the state's witnesses. Nevertheless, I managed to secure an acquittal for Donnie on the day of the verdict. In hindsight, I suspect it was more the fairness of the magistrate and the state's lack of evidence that got him acquitted than my mastery of litigation.

With Mafylan out on bail and Donnie acquitted, I was seen as a legal fixer. Not long thereafter, I received a call from Bal to visit Jarro 'Hopjan' Reed, a high-ranking member of the 28s. By now, I was a regular visitor to Pollsmoor Prison. Unlike Mafylan and Donnie, Hopjan was a 'dik ding' (a big man), as I could tell from his tattoos and the way he 'sabella'd' (used the gang language). The charges against Hopjan were as long as his previous string of convictions: kidnapping and torture, arson, murder, possession of an unlawful firearm, and intimidation.

Like the others, he was respectful. 'Meneer,' he said, 'die mense fabricate net charges tienaan my. Hulle wil my net innie tronk hou.' (Sir, these people are just fabricating charges against me. They just want to keep me in jail.) Had it not been for his tattoos and his sabella, I would've sworn that Hopjan wouldn't hurt a fly. I struggled to keep up with my notes as he talked about the charges. Two stood out: kidnapping and torture, and the arson charges. Hopjan had allegedly kidnapped a rival gang member and drilled holes into his kneecaps. When I asked if it was true, he looked at me and giggled softly. 'Dis wat hulle sê, meneer.' (That's what they say, sir.) As for the arson charge, the police alleged he'd set fire to a magistrates' court building because he wanted to get rid of the police docket that implicated him.

I knew this would be a tough one, and by then I was close to burn-out and in urgent need of help. Fate proved to be on my side when I received an unexpected call from Kevin Kiewitz, an old university friend with whom I hadn't spoken in years.

'I heard you'd set up your own practice,' he said, his voice expectant. 'I finished my articles and want to know if there is space for me at your practice.'

'When do you want to start?'

Kevin reported for duty that week and we cemented our partnership, naming our firm Abrahams Kiewitz. I was all too happy to hand him most of my criminal matters, including Hopjan's.

However, the tide was turning against gangsters and drug dealers on the Cape Flats. On the evening of 4 August 1996, images of Rashaad Staggie being burnt alive were beamed to television screens across South Africa and the world. Staggie was a self-proclaimed drug lord and gang leader, and the anti-drug movement PAGAD (People Against Gangsterism and Drugs) had marched to his house to hand him an ultimatum to stop his drug peddling. During the fracas that developed, he was attacked, shot in the head and set ablaze with a petrol bomb. It ignited a deadly war against drug dealers and gangsters, and Stanfield became the next target.

PAGAD decided to march to his posh home in the leafy suburb of Rondebosch. Trouble loomed. I knew Stanfield wouldn't roll over in surrender. As anticipated, he mustered all his forces from Valhalla Park, and on the night of the PAGAD march, a stand-off ensued that placed the entire neighbourhood on tenterhooks. It required police intervention before PAGAD conceded to retreat. This was only the beginning of Stanfield's troubles.

A few weeks later, I received a call to go to his Rondebosch home. When I got there, the road leading to his house was blocked off by police. After explaining the reason for my visit, I was allowed onto the property. Inside, police were swarming through the immaculately furnished rooms of the double-storey house, searching through his personal belongings.

Francois Potgieter, Stanfield's long-standing lawyer, and Advocate Anton Veldhuizen (later Judge Veldhuizen) were already on the scene. Stanfield stood beside them.

'Dankie dat meneer gekom het.' (Thank you, sir, for coming.) He was visibly upset. 'Die fokken boere search my hys vi' kak. Ek wietie wat hulle soekie.' (The fucking police are searching my house for shit. I don't know what they're looking for.)

I'd not seen him this angry before. I spoke briefly to Potgieter and Veldhuizen, and the three men asked me to remain present until the search was completed. From the way the police went about their task, it was clear there was no great hurry.

During the search, a small locked cupboard under the staircase attracted the attention of the captain in charge. The police called in a locksmith. Stanfield became agitated, but maintained his cool. When the cupboard was opened, money tumbled out in stacks of two-hundred-, one-hundred- and fifty-rand bank notes. There were gasps of shock and smiles from the police, but Stanfield remained stone-faced. After a long and arduous count, the tally was in excess of a million rand.

Stanfield was arrested and taken into custody for alleged drug dealing. I accompanied him. It was an evening of high drama, and for the first time, I saw the strong, mighty Stanfield break down in tears. 'Wat de fok dinkie fokken boere van my? Wat moet my kinners van my dink?' (What the fuck do these fucking police think of me? What must my children think of me?) But no sooner had his tears dried than his anger and rage turned to PAGAD. 'PAGAD se ma se poes! Hulle gaat sien wat ek ga' doen. Die ma se poese.' (PAGAD's mother's cunt! They will see what I'm going to do. The mothers' cunts.)

The next few weeks were a battle to get Stanfield out on bail. He was charged with tax fraud and dealing in Mandrax. A lengthy bail hearing ensued, with senior intelligence police officials testifying against him.

'Stanfield has been on our radar since 1978, when he was convicted of illegally selling alcohol,' said Captain Andries Rossouw of the South African Narcotics Enforcement Bureau. 'In 1988, at the request of the President's Council, a special investigating file was opened against him, as he'd turned to selling drugs.'

His testimony was followed by that of Sergeant Leonard Falck of the Organised Crime Unit, who said, 'Since 1994, I've listened to Stanfield's telephone conversations. I suspect him to be involved in huge-scale drug dealing.'

I patiently sat through the proceedings as Advocate Veldhuizen put up a spirited fight to get Stanfield out on bail. I wondered, however, about the issue of morality. If the allegations were true, should Stanfield have known better? Over the next few days, my mind grappled with this moral question. How were we as moral agents supposed to conduct our lives under a system such as apartheid, which had no moral legitimacy? Could we simply do as we wished?

My own questionable moral decisions came to mind. Long before I became a lawyer, I had readily bought stolen goods from the local tsotsis (hoodlums) who'd often gone on a shopping spree of break-ins and muggings in the white suburbs across the railway line. They redistributed their loot for cheap in the township. I'd never considered the force or bloodshed that might have been used to acquire the items, just as it may not have crossed the minds of most white people that we bore the brunt of apartheid so that they could enjoy its privileges.

Whatever Stanfield's choices and moral culpability, growing up on the Cape Flats left most, if not all of us, morally stained. Daily decisions were fraught with moral dilemmas. Religion served as a moral guide for many, while for others, such as Stanfield, a line from John Milton's *Paradise Lost* could have been considered their lodestar: 'Better to reign in Hell than serve in Heaven.'

Stanfield got bail on appeal, but his legal woes were far from over.

18

Life giveth and life taketh away

The year 1996 ended and it was time to celebrate. Despite the turbulent start to my practice, client numbers were up at Abrahams Kiewitz and the demand for our services had increased. For the first time in my life, I could breathe a sigh of financial relief. My survivalist days were finally over, as the practice generated enough income to sustain me, Kevin and our families.

With four days to go before Christmas, we closed the office and headed to the city in a celebratory mood, looking for a nice jol. On Long Street, we stumbled upon a seedy pub playing live music and got more than we'd bargained for – it was a strip joint. The smoke-filled dive was packed with chattering patrons and skimpily dressed waitresses whisking drinks and food among the tables. Our waitress escorted us to a corner table. We settled in, and on stage an exotic dancer twirled up and down a silver pole, removing her clothes piece by piece to the beat of the music. Eventually she hung suspended, completely naked. We laughed heartily, ate, danced and sang along. It's surprising how quickly you forget your principles when you find yourself morally compromised. It didn't occur to me to question whether the dancer's naked display was an act of women's liberation or a case of male exploitation. I just enjoyed the moment. After an afternoon filled with music, eating and laughter, Kevin and I left on a high note.

When we pulled up to my parents' house, Francois was standing outside with Mara and Roseline. They looked sombre, and an eerie feeling came over me. Mara's eyes were red and Roseline wiped away tears.

'Charles, ons het slegte nuus,' Francois muttered. (We have bad news.)

'Wat is dit?' I asked anxiously. (What is it?)

'Mommy het geloop.' (Mommy has walked.)

'Wat bedoel jy?' I shouted, my heart pounding. (What do you mean?)

'Sy's dood.' (She's dead.)

'No! No! No!' My heart sank and my legs buckled. 'It can't be. Tell me it's not true,' I begged Francois, pulling at his shirt.

'It's true. And Eric is also gone.' He held me as his tears flowed.

My head spun and everything around me blurred. I collapsed on the ground.

The previous evening, my mother, father, Anneline, Lorenzo and his friend Eric had travelled to Aberdeen to attend my cousin's wedding. My mother had looked forward to the trip, as she hadn't seen her family in years. A few kilometres before Aberdeen, my father lost control of the vehicle. My mother and Eric died in the accident.

News of the tragedy spread quickly and people travelled from near and far to express their shock and give their condolences. As comforting as their words were, they did little to ease the pain. Our only pillar of strength had been ripped from us. It was an evening of sorrowful wailing as I tried to come to terms with my mother's untimely death.

The bodies arrived in Cape Town the following day and the torment of preparing my mother's funeral began. We decided to cremate her remains the day before Christmas. Being the eldest, Mara, Francois and I shared the responsibility of arranging this. My father cut a lonely figure during this time, occasionally begging for forgiveness.

'I'm so sorry. I didn't mean to lose control.'

But Francois would have none of that. 'You killed her! You killed her!' he raged at him.

I restrained him; now was not the time.

The cremation was a sombre affair. The tributes poured in and it was a fitting farewell, but dark clouds loomed; Francois had it in for my father. When the crowds thinned out, I left for Merilyn's home to get some rest, but I'd hardly put my head down when I heard footsteps approaching rapidly. It was Merilyn in a panic. 'Charles! Charles! Come quickly! Francois is hitting your father!'

The cloudburst had happened sooner than I'd expected. The lounge was in turmoil, as if lightning had struck. Family members and close friends were crying and yelling as Francois laid into my father. He was like a raging beast.

'Stop! Stop! Stop beating me!' my father begged. From the fierce look on his face, Francois had no intention of stopping as he landed one blow after the other.

My immediate reaction was to intervene, but something inside me held back. Francois had been waiting for this moment ever since that day my father had beaten my mother to a pulp when we were little. The hatred I'd seen on his face more than twenty years before had never disappeared; it had lain in wait for this day. My father cried as the blows fell.

'Charles! Do something!' others yelled. 'Stop Francois!' Eventually, I complied. I didn't want Francois to assault him as badly as my mother had been.

'Moet my nie keer nie, Charles. Ek het al lank al vir hierie oomblik gewag.' (Don't stop me, Charles. I've waited a long time for this moment.)

'I know,' I said, pulling him away. 'But stop it. Enough.'

Francois stormed out of the house. My father lay on the floor, sobbing.

I'd witnessed many unpleasant feuds in our house, but this one was cathartic. I felt a sense of relief, yet there was sorrow too. Justice had been served, but at a steep price. My mother was dead, Francois got his revenge, and my father was bruised and battered. When I looked at him, I saw but a shadow of his former self: the mighty patriarch cut to pieces. Ironically, he'd slumped in the corner where the couch had once stood. That was the spot where my mother had almost drowned in her own blood after his merciless cruelty.

'Why didn't God take my life and keep your mother's?' he wept. 'I should have been the one who died. God can take me away.'

I couldn't help but feel sorry for him as I helped him to the couch. I sat down next to him like I'd sat with my mother when the two of them quarrelled. It was time to talk. As with my mother, I had many questions for my father.

'Why the violence and abuse against Mommy all these years?' I asked.

He took a while to respond, and then began with the story of how he'd grown up dirt poor with a stepfather who'd never accepted him. His stepfather had called him 'kaffirkind' and abused both him and his mother. They'd spent many nights sleeping on the streets after fleeing him in terror.

I'd heard this all before, but listened nonetheless. Then my father shared something new. His mother had gone blind, and he didn't know if it was because of all the beatings she'd suffered, the poverty she'd endured or the eleven other children she'd given birth to. Until then, I hadn't known about my father's step-siblings.

'Hulle's almal dood van armte en TB-siekte,' he said tearfully. 'Sommige ná hul geboorte, en anners as kinnes.' (They all died of poverty and TB. Some just after birth, others as children.) Only one had survived – Uncle Pietie.

I was at a loss for words, but I pushed him to explain why, after every-thing he'd been through, he'd chosen to treat my mother with violence.

His response was woeful. 'I grew up with violence and abuse. That's all I ever knew.'

'Yes, as a child!' I snapped. 'But growing up, working and going to church was supposed to change all of that.'

He looked at me, his eyes wide. He paused and then mumbled, 'Ek wiet, ma' selfs by die wêk was djy soes 'n kind behandel. Ek vat my skuld. Ek het fouteer.' (I know, but even at work you were treated like a child. I was at fault. I erred.)

He'd said a lot in a few words. Unable to shake off his own violent and abusive past, he had allowed it to follow him into his adult life and made my mother suffer, while also living a deeply religious life. My feelings towards him were complex and confused. I felt sadness, pity and anger all at the same time. Here was a man who'd devoted his life to the church, provided for his family, given his last to the fellow poor, yet had committed the cruellest acts towards his wife.

Over the next few weeks, as I came to terms with my mother's death, I tried to make sense of this conversation with my father. I realised I'd been born into a bloodline steeped in poverty and soaked in violence. I had no idea how far into the past it stretched. Did it start with time immemorial or did it date back to the arrival of the first settlers in the

Cape and the subsequent butchery of the Khoikhoi, whose blood runs deep in my family's veins? Was it the way my forebears had been enslaved that unleashed the violence? Or, under apartheid, had it metastasised like a stage-four cancer and eaten into my family's fibre? Whatever it was, I vowed from that day to break the scourge of poverty and violence afflicting my family even though the task wouldn't be easy. The sustained income I got from my practice had already moved me out of that poverty gap, and I assisted the family wherever I could.

19

London calling

The time for mourning ended and I went back to work. Life was different. With the little money Kevin and I had saved, we bought a house a few streets away and converted it into our new offices. We also employed our first three support staff members: Edna, a retired schoolteacher, and Melissa and Turcia, two young women who'd recently completed matric.

Sometime in the middle of that year (1997), I received an unexpected fax from my former employer, the Legal Resources Centre, inviting me to apply for the Edward Quist-Arcton Scholarship Award to London. If successful, I would spend three months with British barristers at Cloisters Chambers to gain an understanding of the English legal system. It was just what I needed to lift my spirits. I promptly applied.

Months passed and I was convinced that I had been unsuccessful. Then I received a fax that turned the unexpected into great expectation: my application had been accepted and I would be the first Edward Quist-Arcton scholar. I didn't know whether to laugh or cry, but I was ecstatic. All of a sudden, my world looked different. I was going to embark on my first overseas trip.

I left on 4 January 1998. Family, colleagues and friends accompanied me to the airport to say their goodbyes. After a stopover in Cairo, I arrived at Heathrow Airport the following evening. The environment buzzed with foreign languages and posh English accents. I looked around me, trying to take in as much as I could.

My hosts, Stephen and Helen Solley, were waiting for me in the arrivals hall.

'You must be Charles Abrahams! Welcome to London!' the large, bespectacled Stephen said in superb Queen's English.

'Welcome! Pleased to meet you,' said Helen, a brunette with a high-pitched voice. As we made our way to the city, Stephen wasted no time in telling me his background. 'My father, Leslie, was a leftist barrister and I followed in his footsteps. He was also heavily involved in politics.' With these few words, I felt at ease. I knew I was in good company. 'And you, young man? Tell me about your family.'

With such a difficult and fractious upbringing, I didn't know what to say, but seized on Stephen's father's leftist background. 'I come from a large working-class family,' I said. 'My father was a truck driver and my late mother was an assistant nurse.'

Before I could continue, he interjected: 'I'm sure we'll have lots to say about working-class politics.'

'Yes! Certainly!' I said enthusiastically, and the discussion turned to law and politics.

Helen intermittently pointed out important landmarks and places around London. 'That's Trafalgar Square,' she said, indicating four prominent lion statues. I hardly remembered any names and places as we drove, except when we got to the London borough of Hackney, in the east of the city, where the Solleys lived.

'Welcome to Hackney,' Stephen said. It was too dark for me to see much of the place except for the row of triple-storey homes. Stephen was quick to point out the politics behind their choice of residence. 'Hackney was historically an industrial area and attracted a lot of working-class people. Because of our solidarity with the working class, we chose to live here.'

Their four boys had keenly awaited my arrival and supper was ready. Daniel, short and stocky, was their eldest son; Sam, the tall one, was about my age; and Theo and Louis were younger. They all warmly introduced themselves and we soon sat down to eat. For most of the evening, I was interrogated about life under apartheid and in the new South Africa, and didn't get much opportunity to ask about London. We retreated to bed late that evening.

Everything about the Solley household was different, from the family dinner to the simple goodnight greetings. The atmosphere was so peaceful and quiet that it bothered me. I wondered if something was wrong.

I wasn't used to any of this. The following morning, I woke to silence: no shouting, no screams, no gunshots. It was a strange feeling. I peeped out of the window and saw a lush green common behind the backyard. It was a world totally unlike the one I knew thirteen thousand kilometres away. I made my way downstairs to where Stephen, Helen and the two younger boys were already preparing breakfast. Stephen had arranged for the boys to take me on my first trip on the London Underground, as he wanted to get me London-ready.

To Londoners, New Yorkers and those in certain other world cities, underground commuting is part of daily life, but it was far removed from my Bream Way reality. Our journey started at Mile End and ended at Oxford Circus. Back on ground level, the streets were swarming with people and I stayed close to the Solleys. We spent the day hopping from buses to the Underground as they showed me the length and breadth of the city. Later that afternoon, as we headed home, Louis remarked, 'You should now be London-ready.'

I couldn't wait for my first day at Cloisters Chambers, and I was eager to get to grips with the English judicial system. Tucked away in the tranquil surrounds of Inner Temple, a precinct dating back to the twelfth century and steeped in the history of the medieval Knights Templar, stood 1 Pump Court, Cloisters Chambers. My first introduction was to Stephen's colleague Michael Turner, who co-administered the scholarship with him. 'How wonderful to meet you at last. I'm sure you're going to have a fabulous time at Cloisters,' he said, laughing amiably. Once I'd met everyone, I was settled in a small office with Stephen. My work was already cut out. During the first few weeks, I accompanied trainees and newly qualified barristers to courts in and around London to observe English law in action. The similarity between English and South African law was obvious, given that South Africa had once been a British colony. The ceremonial pomp of barrister gowns, how they entered court with a gracious bow and how they addressed the court as 'My Lord! My Lady!' were meticulously observed protocols.

Yet there were differences. It boggled my mind that Britain's esteemed legal profession could cling to such antiquated relics as wigs, which had nothing to do with the practice of law. It's said that in the seventeenth century, during the reign of Charles II, the wig was regarded as an essential fashion item of polite society. However, given the unhygienic conditions that prevailed at the time, the real use was as protection against hair lice. In some instances, it also compensated for hair loss. Yet even though wig-fashion waned and hygiene improved, barristers and judges stubbornly clung to their wigs. The assumption was that it enforced solemnity and the authority of the law for criminals, just as it kept juries from favouritism based on a barrister's dress. An even more bizarre interpretation was the practical benefit it afforded barristers and judges as a means of disguise to prevent criminals identifying them in the streets and possibly seeking vengeance.

The most significant encounter of my stay in London was meeting the legendary Sir Sydney Kentridge QC, of whom I'd heard and read. Kentridge was a larger-than-life figure in legal circles. Some regarded him as one of the greatest lawyers of the twentieth century. A renowned South African–born English barrister, he had a legal career spanning nearly fifty years. He'd served as Nelson Mandela's lawyer during the Treason Trial in 1958, and had represented Steve Biko's family at the inquest into Biko's death in 1977. After that, he'd worked as a barrister at the English bar. I suspected that Kentridge and his wife, Felicia, herself a lawyer, had had a hand in my Edward Quist-Arcton selection, as both were founding members of the LRC. Stephen and Helen arranged a special dinner with them.

On the evening in question, I expected to meet two elderly lawyers well into retirement. I was wrong. At seventy-six, Sydney was still running a busy daily practice, while Felicia, sixty-eight, had turned to painting. During the conversation, I discovered that they were the parents of renowned artist William Kentridge. As the evening progressed, Stephen asked Sydney, 'So what does a pre-eminent lawyer like you have to say to a young fellow like Charles?'

I looked eagerly at Sydney, hoping to get some high-level legal advice. He looked at me, flicked his eyebrows, smiled and said, 'Enjoy London as much as you can. This is the start of your world experience.'

I was baffled by this response. Before I could say anything, Felicia jumped in. 'Yes, you should also go to the art galleries and museums. There are plenty of them in London.'

Perplexed by their advice, I realised that very little law was on the menu that evening.

Because I was curious to see Kentridge in action, Stephen arranged for me to sit alongside his long-time friend and colleague Judge Stephen Sedley in the Queen's Bench Division the following week, promising that I wouldn't be disappointed. Kentridge was scheduled to appear before Judge Sedley. On the morning of the hearing, a sizeable contingent of lawyers occupied the courtroom, and from the hordes of files in front of them, it was clear the court was in for a legal showdown.

Kentridge was acting for Her Majesty's Government, opposing an application brought by the Turkish Cypriot Association, which sought a judicial review of Britain's decision to promote Cyprus's accession to the European Union. His opponent was Sir Elihu Lauterpacht QC, son of distinguished international law barrister Sir Hersch Lauterpacht QC, widely regarded as the modern-day father of international law. Like father, like son: Elihu had followed in his father's footsteps and become one of the most prominent and successful British international law barristers.

Lauterpacht got straight to the point – Britain was forbidden, in terms of the 1960 Treaty of Guarantee, from participating in any political or economic union with Cyprus. 'The government acted unlawfully in supporting Cyprus in its quest for accession to the European Union,' he submitted. Lauterpacht made his points in such a composed, collected manner that by the end of his two-hour-long submission, he'd convinced me of his arguments and I didn't think Kentridge stood a chance.

Kentridge rose, cleared his throat and, like Lauterpacht, calmly made his submission. 'My Lord, to approach this matter in the manner the applicants did, is to approach it through the looking glass. This is the very type of case that, for well-established legal reasons, British courts should not sit in judgement of.' For almost an hour, Kentridge laid into Lauterpacht's submissions and swiftly disintegrated what had looked like a watertight argument.

Until that day, I'd had little knowledge of international law. Because of South Africa's isolation during apartheid, judges and lawmakers made little of it. Kentridge and Lauterpacht therefore had me captivated. They'd exposed me to a world of international law I'd only sporadically come across in legal textbooks.

It didn't take long for Judge Sedley to deliver his judgment. As I'd expected, he ruled in favour of Her Majesty's Government. My mind was made up; I wanted to know more about international law.

—⁓—

Just when I thought things couldn't get better, Stephen served up his next guest, ninety-one-year-old John Platts-Mills, the former Labour Party politician and barrister. I was in for a treat. Platts-Mills was as strong as an ox, with a crushing grip on his handshake. Stephen had invited him for one purpose – to tell me his life story. After we settled in, Platts-Mills humorously asked, 'So what do you want to know from a ninety-one-year-old old-timer who has had his day?'

'Everything!' I replied.

'I won't bore you with my childhood except to say I was born in 1906 in New Zealand, finished my law degree and left for Oxford in 1928 on a Rhodes scholarship to further study law. In 1932, I was called to the Inner Temple bar as a barrister.'

'Oh, come on, John! Don't be so bloody modest about your achievements,' Stephen interjected. 'You graduated with a double first-class honours from Victoria University and a first-class honours from Oxford. Then there's your string of sporting achievements.'

Platts-Mills chuckled.

Eager to know how he'd landed up in politics, I asked, 'So how did a first-class barrister like you get so deeply involved in politics?'

He stared at me. 'Young man, how well do you know history?' Before I could answer, he continued, 'It all started with that bastard of a general, Francisco Franco, who started a bloody civil war in Spain in 1936. He and his fascist and Nazi allies, the monarchists, religious conservatives and bloody right-wing supporters. These bastards killed the dream of a democratic Spain. I couldn't sit idly by as they did so and slaughtered thousands of innocent civilians. I joined the Labour Party in that year, hoping I could influence Britain's policy of non-intervention.'

I couldn't imagine one person having the power to influence a country's entire foreign policy. Trying to keep the sarcasm from my voice, I asked, 'What made you think you could do so?'

Platts-Mills took a deep breath and a sip of chardonnay. 'If I could be a first-class lawyer I was sure I could be a first-class politician.'

Stephen pressed him further. 'But why your support for communist Russia at a time when there was very little support for it in the West?'

He chuckled at Stephen's question, then replied, more seriously. 'In the aftermath of the tragedy of the First World War, the world needed a new orientation, a more equitable society. The 1917 Russian Revolution provided much hope.'

I sat upright, intrigued. I was eager to know how a new orientation could come about when the world was caught in an obliterating ideological grip.

'As fascism and Nazi Germany flexed its muscle across Europe, I argued that Britain should form a popular front with the Soviet Union to stop the tide. But since we had a conservative, anti-communist government, I wasn't taken seriously.'

'So why did Britain change its attitude towards Russia?' I asked.

'My good old friend, Sir Richard Cripps, who was the British ambassador to Moscow, called me one morning and told me Winston Churchill wanted to see me. By then, Russia had already entered the Second World War against Nazi Germany and Churchill wanted me to change Russia's image in the eyes of the British public.

'I met with Churchill and agreed to his request. I helped form Soviet friendship committees in Britain and frequently travelled between London and Moscow, meeting with Joseph Stalin and Churchill.'

I was surprised at the casual manner in which John spoke about these meetings. Like many, I'd only learnt of Churchill and Stalin as important historical figures: Churchill, the great Second World War British prime minister, and Stalin, the Russian leader credited with Russia's rapid industrialisation after the Second World War, but also with causing the deaths of millions of his own people. Here was Platts-Mills, a first-class barrister, hobnobbing with the two. Unbelievable. And there was more to come.

'After Nazi Germany was defeated, the Allied forces retreated to their old anti-communist rhetoric, but I stood firm. In my view, we needed a better world and closer relationships with Russia.'

Stephen, growing impatient, urged him to talk about Stalin's death.

'Oh yes! When Stalin died in 1953, the Kremlin invited me to attend his funeral as one of his pallbearers. Only a handful of people from the West were allowed to attend.'

At that point I realised I was in the presence of living history. Platts-Mills's story confirmed my belief that it is possible to combine law and politics for the greater social good. I saw in him everything I wanted to be – a lawyer using law as a tool to transform society for a better life for all.

But not everything in London was about law and politics. I took the Kentridges' advice and spent most of my weekends visiting art galleries and museums, and I extended my cultural reach to opera. Most memorable was my trip to the Royal Opera House to see Handel's *Giulio Cesare*. I'd never been to the opera before. Immaculately dressed, Stephen, Helen and I took our seats towards the middle of a spectacularly appointed auditorium. The audience, mostly white, appeared at ease in these surroundings and chatted gaily.

The glossy little opera booklet Helen bought helped a lot by summarising the plot: it is the year 48 BC in Egypt and Caesar has arrived triumphant after defeating Pompey. Cornelia and Sextus, Pompey's wife and son, ask Caesar to spare Pompey's life, but it's too late, and Caesar is presented with Pompey's head in a casket. Cornelia laments her husband's death while Sextus swears to avenge him. Disturbed by Pompey's death at the hands of Ptolemy, the ruler of Egypt, Caesar sets out to find him. But Ptolemy's sister, Cleopatra, has her sights on the crown and wins favour with Caesar. Ptolemy's rule is over.

Silence fell as soon as the lights faded and the curtains opened. I was as excited as the rest of the audience when Caesar entered the stage with his army to be met by Cornelia and Sextus, but when they began to sing, my excitement waned. I tried to follow the scene as a general arrived with Pompey's head, but the operatic voices kept distracting me and I gave up trying to make sense of it. The different tones and voices were too much for me. Stephen and Helen were gripped and so was everyone else, with some glued to their binoculars, but no matter how hard I tried to feel moved, I remained impervious to the rendition on stage. I couldn't tell whether it was simply a matter of cultural difference or whether years of gunshots and the scraping of machetes on tarmac had deafened my ears to anything new. Towards the end of the performance, I did find resonance when Cleopatra betrayed Ptolemy, who was killed by Sextus, and Caesar proclaimed his love for her. Perhaps the killing was easier to relate to. Together with the audience, I rose to applaud.

My time in London drew swiftly to its end, and I spent my last week at the Stephen Lawrence inquiry. Lawrence, a teenager, had been senselessly knifed to death in April 1993 by five white youths, simply because he was black. It felt as if I was back home. Everything was so similar, from police bungles and incompetence to cover-ups and what many suspected was deep-rooted racism within the Metropolitan Police Service.

By the time I left London, the inquiry was into its second week and would only finish its work the following month. Its findings were scathing of the police and recommended widespread changes to police operations. Despite this sombre end note, my experience in London marked a turning point in my life. My incredible hosts, Stephen and Helen, together with Sydney Kentridge and John Platts-Mills, had set my world alight. And it was about to get even hotter.

20

Seduction in Wiesbaden

A year earlier I'd met a young German woman who'd worked as a volunteer at a children's organisation in Cape Town. Because of her politics, we soon struck up a friendship. She belonged to Autonomen, a left-wing sociopolitical movement that had formed in the aftermath of the 1968 student-led protests in Paris. Autonomen consisted of a mixed bag of feminists, ecologists, anarchists and anti-imperialists, and she was driven by the organisation's stirring spirit to forge new identities of international solidarity. She had spent most of her young adult life in Autonomen and had been living in a commune at the time of the fall of the Berlin Wall and the subsequent collapse of the Soviet Union. These events had been a crushing blow for her and Autonomen, and South Africa, post-1994, had given her a few months of respite.

From London I flew to Germany and arrived at Frankfurt airport in the afternoon. There she was, Simone – blonde, petite, with glittering green eyes. We couldn't conceal our emotions as we warmly hugged one another, and we hardly stopped talking on the drive to her home in Wiesbaden. Occasionally, I gazed at the picturesque green landscape and forests along the highway. It was beautiful.

We arrived at Simone's apartment off Dotzheimer Strasse, on the first floor of a former industrial building. It was small – a tiny bedroom, lounge and bathroom – but superbly decorated. I made myself comfortable on the sleeper couch in the lounge. She'd already made plans for me to meet some of her friends and Autonomen comrades – Wolfgang, Jurgen, Silja and Giacomo – for supper.

I'd expected a politically charged evening. Instead, it turned out to be a smoke-filled occasion of beer and laughter as Jurgen talked about the cars he fixed for customers and Silja about the happiness her little daughter brought her. Only Giacomo, who barely spoke English, ventured into politics. With Simone interpreting, he explained that he was Italian and had come to Germany in the late 1980s as a left-wing political activist.

'The Italian military police, the Carabinieri, wanted to arrest me.' He spoke German with a heavy Italian accent. 'They thought I was a member of the outlawed Brigate Rosse [Red Brigade], but I'm not.'

Silja couldn't resist teasing him. 'Don't believe him, he is a member of the Red Brigade. That's why he's here.'

Everyone laughed. Silja's playfulness made me realise I was being too serious for the enjoyable, laid-back evening and that I needed to relax.

I'd given myself four weeks off work for this holiday, so I decided to let loose – perhaps a bit too loose – and savour everything Wiesbaden had to offer. Simone and I visited the famous Rheingau region, the breathtaking Neroberg, the Russian Orthodox Church and even the fairy-tale Lorelei rock that evoked my childhood tales of beautiful mermaids seducing sailors. Then a visit to a local spa changed everything. The last thing I had on my mind was landing up stark naked in a sauna among bodies of all shapes, sizes and colours, men and women all together, slogging it out in intense heat. Gobsmacked, I put on a brave face, pretending to feel normal. I didn't. Just a few years earlier, it had been totally forbidden for South African men of colour to even glimpse the naked body of a white woman. This was a taboo so entrenched in apartheid ideology that black men dared not touch the 'sacred' bodies of white women. But I kept up the pretence and smiled at Simone, who sat next to me. Her body was adorable.

That evening, as we retired to our separate beds, there was an awkwardness in the air. I was restless and couldn't stop thinking about the spa. Simone couldn't sleep either. After an uneasy lull, she broke the silence.

'What are you doing?'

Foolishly I responded, 'Are you speaking to me?'

'Who else?'

'I can't sleep,' I admitted.

'Me too.'

I decided to interpret her reply as a cue. I plucked up my courage, got out of bed and headed for her bedroom, entering with my heart throbbing.

I sat down next to her on the futon. The bedside lamp cast a dim light. 'What's bothering you?'

She looked at me, puzzled. 'What do you mean? Nothing bothers me.'

I realised I'd completely misjudged the situation. Red-faced, I got up, apologising profusely. 'I'm really sorry. I thought something was bothering you.'

Just as I was about to leave, Simone smiled and said, 'Where're you going? I was just teasing you. Come sit here.'

I obliged.

After a moment of awkward silence, everything changed, fast. Before I knew it, we were in each other's arms, passionately kissing. We dropped onto the bed in a tight embrace. I'd kissed the lips of many women, but never the lips of a white woman. For the next few minutes we didn't speak; we just allowed our embrace to take its natural course. Occasionally, the futon base squeaked as we rolled from corner to corner, our bodies entwined. Eventually, we lay unmoving in one another's arms.

Every taboo ingrained in me through decades of apartheid brainwashing and indoctrination was disintegrated by this single act of intimacy. It was as if a hoax had finally been exposed for what it was – a mere hoax. The sex was great, but it was no different from my experiences with Merilyn and other women. Within the excitement, I felt cheated that apartheid could have perpetrated such horrible fraud.

But the following morning the atmosphere was different. It wasn't just spring in the air; love was in full bloom. Simone and I were full of kisses, and in the weeks that followed, we couldn't keep our hands off one another. However, I was still in a relationship with Merilyn, so by the time my holiday ended I was emotionally torn. I was madly in love with Simone and had no idea what I'd got myself into. Too tired to figure out how to deal with it, I left for Cape Town a deeply compromised man.

21

Revelations in Amsterdam

'Welcome Back! We Missed You!' read the banner at the surprise welcome-home party Merilyn had arranged. She was more than excited to see me.

'I really missed you,' she said as she hugged and kissed me.

It was awkward, but in the excitement I was able to conceal my inner turmoil. 'I missed you too,' was my somewhat lacklustre reply. Family members bayed for details of my London experience. I shared most of it, but was sparse with the specifics of my time in Germany. Merilyn knew Simone from her time in Cape Town and didn't make much of my visit to her.

I eased back into my work routine in the days that followed, but found it difficult to get going. Having had a taste of Europe, I found Nooitgedacht small and parochial. I wanted to go back to study international law and be with Simone. For months, I spent most of my time at work trawling the internet for study opportunities. My absence from home didn't sit well with Merilyn.

'Since you're back from Europe, it's just work and work,' she complained. 'What's going on?'

I didn't have the courage to tell her of my plans, let alone my affair with Simone. Instead, I concocted one excuse after the other, mostly about catching up on work.

A few months later, a small newspaper ad caught my attention: Leiden University in the Netherlands had invited applicants to apply for the 1999/2000 LLM programme in public international law. I seized the opportunity and applied.

Meanwhile, Simone and her friend Karin had decided to visit me in Cape Town. My clandestine relationship was about to be busted. Unsure how to break the news to Merilyn, I opted for a woolly story about how Germans love Cape Town and always come back. It worked so well that a few days after their arrival, I felt confident enough to organise a small social event at a restaurant with a few friends to welcome Simone and Karin.

The evening started off well; even Merilyn and Simone were happily chatting to one another. I'd assured Simone that I'd spoken to Merilyn about our relationship and that she was okay with it. I thought I had it all in the bag, but an hour or so into the evening, Merilyn cornered me. 'Take me home, right now!'

Everyone turned to stare.

'What happened?' I asked, pretending to be surprised. It was a question I shouldn't have asked.

'You have the audacity to ask me what happened? You damn well know what happened.'

To save face and further embarrassment, I ushered her out. By the time we got to the car, Merilyn was enraged.

'How could you! How could you, Charles?'

I didn't know what to say. 'I tried to tell you,' I said hesitantly.

'Tell me what? You didn't tell me anything! How long has this been going on behind my back? Now I know why you've spent all the time at the office. It was with her!' She broke down in tears.

I was at a loss for words. I felt wretched, not sure what to do. Even though we'd had the usual lovers' quarrels in the past, this was devastating. That night, our seven-year relationship took a beating.

Merilyn was emotionally distraught for the next few days and we didn't speak a word to each other. I'd never seen her hurt so badly. But despite the grief I'd caused her, my mind was made up; I was resolute about my relationship with Simone. Even though she was furious that I hadn't told Merilyn the truth, the incident didn't dampen her spirits, and by the time her visit ended, we'd already planned our next get-together.

Merilyn and I grudgingly continued with our wounded relationship. I didn't have the stomach to break up with her and, in any case, it didn't feel right to abandon my relationship with her for a woman who was white and European. Merilyn clearly didn't want to let go either. So I found myself in an open relationship with two women, something I'd not thought possible a few months earlier.

Time passed quickly, and a few months later, Simone and I set off to the Italian city of Naples to visit her friend Giacomo, who'd returned to his homeland. The trip afforded me an opportunity to develop my world experience and cement my relationship with Simone. For Merilyn, it was adding salt to an open wound.

My trip, however, was overshadowed by a telephone call from my business partner, Kevin. Rowdy as usual, he couldn't contain his excitement. 'Great news, Charles! You've been accepted to study at Leiden University.' I was speechless with happiness. Life couldn't have been better and I couldn't wait to get back to Cape Town to prepare for my new life as a student in the Netherlands.

—⚹⚹—

Once home, my excitement waned and reality caught up. Even though I'd been accepted into the LLM programme, I had no idea how I would pay for my studies. Abrahams Kiewitz was doing well, but it didn't generate enough money to finance studies abroad for a year. Unless I secured a bursary, the opportunity would be lost. I immediately went into pleading mode, sending letters to whomever I thought suitable. It was an exercise in futility. One by one the responses came back: 'We regret to advise that we are unable to assist.' Time was running out and I was about to give up when I made one last-ditch effort and turned to Chief Justice Arthur Chaskalson. He called me a few weeks later. To say I was nervous would have been an understatement. His voice was soft and calm as if to break bad news.

'I spoke to Professor John Dugard this morning,' he said. 'I'm told you've been nominated for the Nelson Mandela Scholarship.'

I could have shat my pants.

I had no idea who had nominated me, but at that moment I was overcome with emotion. I thanked the chief justice I don't know how many times. It turned out that, earlier in the year, President Nelson Mandela had received an honorary doctorate from Leiden University and the university had established the scholarship in his honour. South African law professor John Dugard, who was also the visiting international law professor at Leiden University, served on the committee that made the final decision.

A few weeks later, I received confirmation of the scholarship. Many congratulations streamed in, but had my mother been alive, I know she would have said it was God's will.

—⟋𝕞⟍—

I arrived in Leiden on 5 September 1999, a cool autumn day. Bicycles whizzed past as I made my way to the student residence along cobbled streets lined with fluttering golden-brown leaves. The residence was already brimming with student life. I had a week before the academic year commenced, and used the time to get to know the city and meet fellow students. We were truly a global mix, with students from Europe, the United States, Honduras, Morocco, Japan, Uganda, Bulgaria and Russia. Most were in their early twenties. At thirty-one, I felt old.

I couldn't have chosen a better time to study international law: the International Court of Justice (ICJ) had its hands full with cases in the aftermath of the Kosovo War. The two international criminal tribunals, the International Criminal Tribunal for the Former Yugoslavia (ICTY) and the International Criminal Tribunal for Rwanda (ICTR), which were set up to prosecute war crimes in the Balkans and genocide and other serious crimes committed in Rwanda respectively, were both in full swing. With the International Criminal Court (ICC) in the making, we had our work cut out, and who better to teach us than Professor John Dugard?

Professor Dugard's lectures on the legality of NATO's use of force in Kosovo without the approval of the United Nations Security Council were a hit with students. These lectures evoked a fierce debate, with the class evenly divided between those for and against NATO's intervention. The debate also pitted American and European students against

Russian students, with accusations that Russia had committed war crimes in Chechnya. But it was Dugard's views on Israel that courted the most controversy. To him, Israel was a criminal state whose crimes were infinitely worse than apartheid South Africa's. His views didn't sit well with some in the class, who argued for Israel's right to exist and defend itself. My personal experience of living under a criminal apartheid state provided much thoughtful insight to the majority, who were unsure of their legal views on Israel.

Meanwhile, Simone and I developed a routine. We saw each other every second weekend: she'd come to Leiden one weekend and I'd travel to Wiesbaden two weekends later. Our love blossomed. The weekends we didn't see each other, I spent in Leiden. During this time I discovered the city's vibrant student life, something I hadn't known during my undergraduate years because I'd completed my studies part-time. I soon struck up a friendship with Mark Horrelt, a Canadian student. We didn't have much in common except for our ages. Mark was a few years older than me, and with his Pierce Brosnan looks, he was a magnet for the female students.

It didn't take us long to outgrow Leiden and set our sights on Amsterdam. I'd always harboured a youthful fantasy about the wickedness of this old sailors' city and couldn't wait to experience its vices. On my weekends off, Mark and I would head to Amsterdam and hop from bar to bar until the wee hours of the morning. Coming from Nooitgedacht, it was quite an experience to see Mark confidently approaching a strange woman and chatting her up. Most of the time that's where our paths split: he gained a woman and I did not. But he'd always encourage me.

'Chuck,' as he called me, 'don't be shy, I know you can do it.'

I tried not to think about Simone.

One evening, at a student house party, I couldn't resist the temptation to chat up a shy blonde I'd been eyeing the whole evening. Summoning my courage, I walked up to her and asked for a dance. From the look in her eyes, I thought I was about to be dissed. Fortunately, her nervous giggle broke the ice. She had no idea how relieved I was. Once on the dance floor, we couldn't stop, and by the time the party was over, I'd got all her details. She was Verna, an Austrian student also pursuing an LLM degree at Leiden. We agreed to meet the following day for coffee and from there we developed a secret love affair.

My new-found confidence didn't stop there. My trips with Mark had awoken a vile, dark force inside me that had lain fallow for heaven knows how long, and I began making solitary trips to Amsterdam to visit the city's seedy sex shops and cinemas. During one of my first trips, I landed up at a cheap twenty-four-hour X-rated cinema. It was dark and stuffy inside, and the air was filled with sex. On the screen, a woman moaned loudly as she sucked a penis while being penetrated by two overweight men. I took my seat in the back row, stunned. I could hear a couple having sex a few seats away while a guy in front jerked off. I found it all arousing, defying sexual and moral boundaries I didn't think I'd cross. I left, and set in motion future solitary trips.

I could hardly wait for my Friday evenings off. As soon as I stepped off the train, I was a different person, shorn of inhibitions. Repressed feelings had been awoken. Soon, I was prowling the city's narrow cobbled streets, seeking out its most lewd and sordid sex shops, targeting them one by one. I'd spend hours browsing pornographic material, engrossed in the most degenerate fantasies: everything from straight, gay and bisexual to dominatrices and sadomasochism.

Pent up, hot and bothered, I'd make my way to the famous Red Light District. Here, under the cloak of anonymity, I turned my darkest fantasies into reality. With so many women available, I was spoilt for choice. Unable to make up my mind, I would roam the district like a vulture circling carrion: around Oudekerksplein, along Oudezijds Voorburgwal, into Trompettersteeg. When dissatisfied, I'd walk over Oudekennissteeg Bridge into Oudezijds Achterburgwal, where, if fortune was smiling, there'd be a petite young blonde, her inviting body skimpily dressed in a neon bikini. Initially, I'd walk past the window a few times to make sure she was the one I wanted. She'd catch my eye, invite me in and I would oblige.

We'd barely speak.

'How much?'

'Fifty guilders.'

As soon as the door shut behind me, she would pull the red curtain closed – a sign that she was engaged. I would follow her down a narrow passage into a heated bedroom. Her face would be so innocent, perhaps a mere twenty years old. We would undress. She'd undo her bra, revealing tiny, pointy breasts. Her pubic area would be clean shaven. We'd go through the motions, her eyes closed, mine open. I'd be all over her smooth, white body, enacting the scenes I'd seen in the sex shops. After a while, I'd finish, get dressed and leave.

It was a routine I indulged in over and over again. The district had a variety of women of different backgrounds – African, Asian, Caribbean and Caucasian, to name but a few. I engaged most of them, but my preference was for petite young white women of mostly Eastern European origin.

Occasionally, I deviated from this pattern and visited the city's bars and nightclubs. One evening in a nightclub on Korte Leidsedwarsstraat, I checked out the vibe and headed straight for a brunette at the bar. Making myself comfortable next to her, I casually made my advance.

'I hope you're having an enjoyable time.'

She was at ease, relaxed. 'I'm trying to. What about you?'

With that response, I knew it was on. We spent the night chatting, drinking and dancing until we left the club together. She invited me over to her apartment and we fucked the hell out of each other. The following morning, I left her apartment, exhausted, and began the trip back to Leiden. By then, I'd forgotten her name and was sure she'd long forgotten mine.

But things were about to come to a head. As I sat in the train, aimlessly staring out of the window, I felt sick to the bone. There was something rotten inside me and I couldn't take it any more.

What the fuck is wrong with you? I raged at myself. *Pussy! White pussy! That's all you have on your mind.* I felt deeply ashamed.

I tried to suppress my shame by thinking of Simone, but I found myself drenched in disgust. I'd thought that my relationship with her would dampen my suppressed desire for white women, but I was wrong. I'd underestimated the effects of sexual apartheid. The caricature of white women as apartheid's crown jewels, the progenitors of its survival, had left me with an almost impenetrable scar – a mind constantly yearning to touch and eat of the flesh of the white man's preserve. The more forbidden it was, the more deeply it was ingrained in my mind. It had been naïve of me to think that years of repressed sexual feelings towards white women could be wiped away by my relationship with Simone.

But an even greater damage, unspoken of since childhood, had festered in the dark. For too long, I'd pretended it wasn't there, but the more I sought sexual relief in Amsterdam's sleazy alleyways, the more it brought me closer to the shame of my past. And then that train journey to Leiden took me back to my childhood.

22

#MeToo

If I'd known what was in store for me the day I kicked the ball into Aunty Hanna's backyard, I would never have leapt over the fence to fetch it.

Francois and I were playing soccer when the miskick happened. I was about thirteen years old. Once in the neighbour's backyard, I noticed the stoep light burning and went to tell Aunty Hanna she had a light on. Ever since her husband had died a few years earlier, her house had been eerily quiet. Her two young sons, Andrew and Christian, had gone to live with their grandparents in Elim, a small Moravian mission station about two hundred kilometres from Cape Town.

'Aunty Hanna!' I shouted, knocking on the door. There was no response. Hesitant, I turned the handle, found the door unlocked and cautiously entered. It was quiet inside. Again, I called out. As I was about to leave, I heard a man's voice: 'Wie's daar?' (Who's there?) I went to the back room, where he must have been sleeping.

'Dis ek,' I said. (It's me.) The room was dark and stuffy. 'Middag, Uncle. Die stoeplig brand?' (Good day, Uncle. The stoep light is on?)

He thanked me. As I was about to leave, he asked my name. I told him.

'I'm Uncle Samuel but you can call me Uncle Sammy. Do you want some Coke?' He reached for the half-empty bottle next to his bed. From the empty Coke bottles around, I figured he must have drunk a lot. 'Come sit here, next to me,' he said.

I took the glass of Coke he offered. His eyes were bloodshot, his cheeks covered in stubble.

'Have more,' he urged me. My eyes were fixed on the leftover sandwiches on the plate next to the empty bottles. 'Are you hungry?' he asked. 'Have them.' He edged closer to me.

As I laid into the Coke and bread, Uncle Sammy's hand unexpectedly touched my thigh. I instinctively pushed his hand away.

'It's okay, don't be afraid,' he assured me, taking a firmer grip on my thigh.

Startled, I stared at him in confusion.

'If ever you're hungry again, just come to me. I'll give you whatever you want,' he said. 'Don't worry, I won't hurt you.' He loosened his grip and caressed my thigh. Puzzled, I pulled back.

He tightened his grip again, then put his hand into my pants and began to stroke my penis. 'Shoo! Shoo!' he hushed me. 'I won't hurt you.' I tried pushing his hand away, but he was too strong. By then, he'd already pulled down his pants and underpants. Naked, he forced me to stroke his penis as he stroked mine.

'Stop it! Stop it!' I shouted. 'You hurt me!'

But I couldn't break Uncle Sammy's grasp. His moans grew louder and it wasn't long before stuff squirted from his penis all over my hand. I yanked my hand away, not knowing what it was.

'Go and wash yourself in the bathroom,' he said. Which I hurriedly did. Afterwards he told me, 'This is our little secret. Don't ever tell anyone about it.' He handed me a fifty-cent coin. 'If you ever need pocket money, come to me. I'll give it to you.'

I walked out of the house, confused: bread, Coke, white stuff and fifty cents.

Francois was furious that I'd taken so long, but I couldn't tell him the secret I shared with Uncle Sammy. Nevertheless, I showed him the fifty cents the uncle had given me. He was happy, as we could buy lots of sweets.

Over the next few weeks, food streamed over the fence.

'Give this to your mother,' Uncle Sammy would say. I obliged, and my mother was overjoyed.

'What a kind person,' she said. Uncle Sammy soon became a household friend. Having won my mother's trust, he asked her if I could sleep over whenever Aunty Hanna went to Elim. My mother was only too happy to agree to this and may have assumed that Aunty Hanna's home provided me with a little relief from our crowded house. I had no doubt that Uncle Sammy knew of the troubles in our house and took advantage of them.

It was during these sleepovers that Uncle Sammy would act out his grotesque fantasies. He'd convinced me that he wasn't doing anything wrong, and my young mind believed him. Looking back, I realise Uncle Sammy exploited two of my greatest vulnerabilities – poverty and youth. I convinced myself that one day this experience would magically disappear and I would never have to think about it again. I was wrong.

Uncle Sammy was always one step ahead. It wasn't just food and money that he used to get his way. He also took me to Elim to visit Andrew and Christian. After all the wonderful stories they'd told me, I couldn't wait to see Elim. Nestled quietly behind the picturesque Overberg mountains in the Western Cape, it had been founded in 1824 by German missionaries and became a place of refuge for impoverished Khoisan and destitute freed slaves in the Cape Colony. Andrew and Christian were proud to tell me of Elim's heritage. The town was home to South Africa's first and only slave monument, erected in 1938 to commemorate the end of slavery in 1834.

Elim was everything I'd imagined – its inhabitants tilled the soil and tended their flocks while children played carefree in the meadows. In the first week of my arrival, I felt as free as those slaves must have felt when they first set foot there. But that freedom didn't last long. One night, as I slept in the tiny room I shared with Andrew and Christian, I felt someone sneak up next to me. At first I thought it was Andrew, but soon realised it was Uncle Sammy. With Andrew and Christian soundly asleep, I put up a desperate fight, but Uncle Sammy had his way. The following morning, Andrew had a smirk on his face.

'Is he also doing it to you?' he asked. I was surprised. Before I could say something, Andrew giggled. 'He always does it. He's done it to us as well.' Not knowing what to say, both of us giggled.

I learnt that Uncle Sammy liked boys and that we were not the only ones he'd assaulted. We thought it funny and made light of it. I had no idea that someone like Uncle Sammy was called a paedophile and considered a serious danger to society.

After a while, I knew I had to escape his clutches, but with our home in turmoil it wasn't easy. I didn't feel that I could turn to anyone for help. I didn't trust the church, my school or the police. At fourteen, I contemplated suicide. One Sunday morning, after a heated quarrel between my mother and father, I blindly ran off until I landed up at the railway station in Bishop Lavis. I hated everything about myself, my family and what was happening to me. I wanted to end it all. 'Today I'm killing myself. I've had enough,' I decided. I cried as I waited for the train. People around me were oblivious to my plans. Then, in the distance, I saw the train approaching. I edged closer to the track. My body was trembling and my palms were sweaty. As the siren wailed, I half-heartedly readied myself for the jump. I closed my teary eyes, but in those few seconds a gush of wind passed me. I didn't have the guts to jump. I retreated to a quiet spot not far from the tracks and sobbed. It would take a further two years before I wrenched myself from Uncle Sammy's clutches, but by then the damage was done.

The year I spent in the Central Library wasn't solely to understand Karl Marx and other philosophers; it was also to come to terms with the damage inside me and to find healing. I was looking to the larger world in the hope of transcending what had happened to me.

My journey continued beyond that year, leading me to works that pulled me in different directions, as was the case with the writings of Viktor Frankl and Elie Wiesel. Both were prominent Holocaust survivors who wrote about their experiences in Nazi concentration camps. If they could survive the Holocaust, I could survive Uncle Sammy. In his acclaimed *Man's Search for Meaning*, Frankl, an Austrian neurologist and psychiatrist, chronicled his confinement to a Jewish ghetto in 1942 and two years later in Auschwitz, where he was to be 'processed', a term used for extermination in the gas chambers. However, instead of expressing hatred for his hopeless situation, he expressed love for his mother and wife. 'The salvation of man is through love and in love', it dawned on him during a frosty early-morning march to a work site in Auschwitz.

Wiesel, a Romanian-born American–Jewish writer and professor, was only fifteen when he and his family landed up in Auschwitz and

Buchenwald. In his book *Night*, he recalls witnessing a truckload of small children being offloaded and burnt. When his father whispers a prayer that ends by asking for God's name to be celebrated and sanctified, an anger rises in Wiesel; God, in this situation, is silent, so what reason is there to thank Him? Unlike Frankl, Wiesel feels a great sense of anger and hatred, and loses his faith in God and human relations.

I could relate to both Wiesel and Frankl's stories. I felt hatred for what Uncle Sammy had done, but felt that I had a better understanding of myself too.

Not surprisingly, I was drawn to existentialism, a philosophy that took hold in the aftermath of the Second World War. Dark and depressing, existentialism is premised on the idea that life has no inherent meaning or purpose, although we can give it meaning once we come into existence. In doing so, we are forced to make choices no matter our circumstances. This, existentialists argue, is the meaning of free will: being free to choose or, as some put it, condemned to be free. I found psychological comfort in existentialism. For the first time I felt I could take my life into my own hands and mould it into the form and purpose I desired.

'Human life begins on the far side of despair,' wrote Jean-Paul Sartre in his drama *The Flies*, which he produced amid the gloom of the Second World War. Sartre is existentialism's greatest proponent and his views made me look at my horrible experiences differently. I found meaning where previously I hadn't, and instead of mere gloom and misery, I saw opportunity, no matter how limited. Kierkegaard, a Danish theologian widely regarded as the first modern-day existentialist, wrote that 'Life can only be understood backwards; but it must be lived forwards.' His view provided me with the ammunition to face my past. I started to weave some of life's big philosophical ideas into my small, daily experiences, producing noticeable changes. Camus provided great wisdom: 'You will never be happy if you continue to search for what happiness consists of. You will never live if you are looking for the meaning of life.' This freed me from that elusive search for happiness, which had haunted me for most of my childhood. I had always seen happiness in other people, but rarely experienced it. After reading

Camus, I realised that I could find happiness within myself no matter how dreadful my circumstances.

But existentialism demands personal commitment. It isn't enough merely to find solace in it; one has to live and act according to its principles. My relationship with Merilyn was the starting point. It marked my mental escape from Uncle Sammy, and Merilyn affirmed my manhood in a way that I sorely needed. With her, I experienced fulfilment and happiness. Yet, despite her love and affection, a void remained, and I gave little in return. I was ashamed of what had happened to me, and most of the time I shut Merilyn out of my life. By the time I met Simone, I was ready to move on.

Amsterdam was a time of insanity caused by the void inside me. It brought me to the abyss and forced me to look myself in the eye and face my torment. I saw in myself not Jekyll and Hyde, but Frantz Fanon's character Jean Veneuse of *Black Skin, White Masks*. Veneuse, a black student of Caribbean origin, falls in love with Andrée, a white French girl, and struggles to come to terms with his own identity – whether he's black or white. A friend convinces him that he is a European at heart, but he feels the need to distinguish himself from the other black men who, from the moment they landed in Europe, had only one thought in mind: to satisfy their appetites for white women. Veneuse claims that

> The majority of them, including those of lighter skin, who often go to the extreme of denying both their countries and their mothers, tend to marry in Europe not so much out of love as for the satisfaction of being the master of a European woman; and a certain tang of proud revenge enters into this.

In marrying Andrée, Veneuse worries that there is no difference between him and the other black men:

> I wonder whether … by marrying you, who are a European, I may not appear to be making a show of contempt for the women of my own race and, above all, to be drawn on by desire for that white

flesh that has been forbidden to us Negroes as long as white men have ruled the world, so that without my knowledge I am attempting to revenge myself on a European woman for everything that her ancestors have inflicted on mine throughout the centuries.

I was confronted with a Jean Veneuse dilemma. Whatever vestiges of apartheid conditioning remained in me, I sought to heal myself through sex with white women. The more I had of it, the more I thought I could be healed. Put crudely, I saw white pussy as a means of curing my black ills and sexual trauma. But just as wanting to be a 'white coloured' couldn't cure my kroes hare, dik lippe, breë neusgate and dark-brown skin, ultimately I felt no different from those 'Negroes' intent on gratifying their lust for white women. Worse still, my behaviour reduced women to objects.

My train journey to Leiden was painful but cathartic, bringing me face to face with the rot and brokenness inside of me. I realised that my healing journey was far from over. However, I already felt better, and none of this stopped me from continuing my relationship with Simone; instead, my love grew stronger. Merilyn came to visit too. Now and then, I'd meet up with Verna or take a trip to the Red Light District.

—⚬—

If contradictions were the hallmark of my personal life, consistency defined my studies. I diligently attended classes and spent endless nights in the university library, doing research and working on my master's thesis. The topic had been decided long before I arrived in Leiden. I'd never forgotten Karl Polanyi's assertion that international finance acted as the main link between politics and economics, which I'd come across in the Central Library when I was nineteen. Now, finally, I had the opportunity to research the financing of apartheid. Leiden's library had an abundance of material proving that foreign banks and corporations had queued to provide loans and credits to the apartheid regime. German and Swiss banks and corporations took the lead, followed by the United States, Britain and France.

My research focused on the legality of these international loans, credits and other forms of finance. Under customary international law, certain debts, commonly referred to as 'odious debts', cannot be transferred to a successor state if it's not in the interest of the majority of its people. I sought to make the case that the post-apartheid democratic state was not liable for the debts of the former apartheid regime, as they were odious and could not have been entered into in the interests of the South African majority. I was so enthused by my research that I sent a copy to President Thabo Mbeki. I never received a response, but I finished the academic year and was awarded a master's degree in public international law.

23

Picking up the pieces

The time came to leave Leiden. Even though I'd grown accustomed to life in Europe, I was looking forward to returning home. It was also a condition of my scholarship that I return to South Africa and plough back the fruits of my education.

A few days before my return, I received an email from Marco, Merilyn's son: 'Charles, could you please buy me a pair of Caterpillar boots or Nike shoes. Oh yes, Brian opposite us hanged himself today in his hokkie.'

Brian had been my childhood friend. I felt numb. Just when I thought I was ready to go home, Bream Way revealed itself in its full goriness, putting a damper on my enthusiasm to return.

Simone tried to persuade me to move to Germany, even proposing marriage. It sounded like a great idea, but it scared me. I'd heard many stories of skilled professionals from the former Soviet Union flocking to Europe after the collapse of the Berlin Wall, only to work in pubs and restaurants, eking out a meagre living. Having struggled all my life to get to where I was, it frightened me that I might land up in Café Klatsch, Simone's favourite pub restaurant, opposite her apartment. Against my desires, I opted to return home.

—⚏—

I arrived in Cape Town on a cold, wet, miserable day. A reluctant Merilyn had agreed to fetch me from the airport. Unlike two years earlier, there was no welcome-home party. No 'I missed you so much' or warm embraces. We greeted each other casually. On our way to the car, a trolley porter recognised me from our school days. 'Charles! My broe, hoe gaanit? Wa' was djy? Was djy osiee?' (Charles! My brother, how are you? Where were you? Where you overseas?)

'I'm okay,' I replied. 'Yes, I was in Holland.'

He had many more questions, excitement glowing in his eyes, but I wasn't in the mood to talk.

The journey home was short and silent. At the traffic lights before entering Nooitgedacht, I instinctively locked my door as a street child approached. I shrugged and mumbled, 'Niks nie, man, sorry.' (Nothing, man, sorry.) It came naturally. On the boundary wall opposite the traffic lights was the graffiti, 'Hosh Ja! 26! Son op! Jou ma se poes!' I felt my blood charging through my veins and my temperature rising. I was back home. Broken windows, fluttering curtains and piled-up rubbish greeted me as we drove past the pink flats. On the left was the primary school I'd attended. The lush green lawns that were once the pride and joy of the school were now rank with weeds. For a moment, my mind returned to Mr Hendricks and the inspector, but I didn't care much about what had happened to them. At the end of the road, we turned left into Olyfberg Way, where a group of children were playing in a rusty abandoned truck next to the vaal flats, oblivious of the world around them. I recognised a few faces and waved. A short drive further and we were in Bream Way.

Even though I'd been gone a year, nothing had changed. The houses, the people, the rubbish and even the stray dogs were still the same. I wondered if I'd made the right decision to return. But it was too late for regrets.

'Aweh, Charles! Long time, no see,' called Kapai, an old school friend. I returned the greeting. Merilyn's dogs, Fluffy, Andy and Mandy, were happy to see me, jostling for an opportunity to jump on me.

Later that afternoon, after a short rest, I went to the office. The women there greeted me warmly. 'Welcome back! Welcome back!' Edna said, and hugged me. Melissa had left and in her place was a bubbly young woman who introduced herself as Anthea. During the year, Turcia had grown into a beautiful twenty-three-year-old. 'It's really nice to have you back,' she said, politely. Kevin was his usual self, 'rof, grof en ombeskof' (rough, gruff and rude), but although he was happy to see me too, his face looked tired.

In the weeks that followed, I resumed working on what remained of Colin Stanfield's referred cases. The picture looked grim. A few months after I'd left for Leiden, Mafylan, the 28 who'd been accused of killing a 26, had died in a revenge attack, his body riddled with bullets. Hopjan, 'die dik ding', was found guilty of kidnapping, torture and arson, and sentenced to eighteen years in prison. But nothing could have prepared me for Donnie, the alleged 28 hitman who I'd got acquitted of murder.

On my way to the office one morning, I heard someone shouting, 'Menee'! Menee'!' I glanced at my rear-view mirror: a man being pushed in a wheelchair was waving at me. I quickly reversed.

'Hello, menee'! Hoe gaanit?' (Hello, sir, how are you?)

It took me a moment to realise it was Donnie. 'What happened to you?' I asked.

He hesitated, looked down and grumbled, 'Djarre, meneer, ek slice mos; 'n petrolbom het in my hanne explode.' (Yeah, sir, it was my fault; a petrol bomb exploded in my hands.)

Both Donnie's hands had been blown off. Shocked at this pitiful sight, I didn't know what to say.

'Het menee' nie soe ietsie da' vi' kossies nie, asseblief?' he begged, holding out his two stumps. (Sir, don't you have a little something there for me for food, please?)

I took out a fifty-rand note and put it in between his stumps. He couldn't thank me enough and waved as I drove off. Shaken, I still couldn't believe what I'd seen. Had karma finally caught up with Donnie?

For Colin Stanfield, life took a more dire turn. During my absence, his woes had continued, and in March 2001 he was sentenced to six years' imprisonment for tax fraud. Hardly two years later, he was diagnosed with incurable lung cancer. After a short release on medical parole, he died on 3 October 2004. For many, Stanfield's death marked the end of a legacy. For others, the legacy continued. Speculation was rife that long before Stanfield's death, his nephew Ralph Stanfield had been prepped to be his successor.

Before I'd gone to Leiden, I'd decided to stop doing criminal work. My decision was prompted by a young woman who approached me on behalf of her brother, who had been taken into custody for murder. The story went that her brother, together with two others, had socialised at a local shebeen in Valhalla Park, where they met a young woman. After a night of heavy drinking, the four left the shebeen together. The following morning, the naked body of the young woman was found on an open field near the shebeen. An autopsy revealed that she'd been raped multiple times and stabbed repeatedly with a broken beer bottle, which was then shoved up her vagina. As I listened to the grisly details, an anger rose in my chest. What had become of us? To what barbarity had we sunk? I decided not to take on the case. It was the end of a short period in criminal law, turbulent yet immensely insightful.

—⚒—

On the domestic front, another period was about to end. I moved out of Merilyn's house and into my own apartment. It was a welcome reprieve, but we chose not to end our relationship. Simone, who'd got used to seeing me regularly while in Leiden, was miserable. It displeased her that I was so far away and she renewed her efforts to lure me back to Germany, but I refused.

We weren't the only ones with love problems. Like many young women, Turcia from the office had pinned her hopes on a prince charming until she discovered that he had fathered a child with another woman. Given our mutual love problems, we sought consolation in each other's misery. It was a big mistake; our self-help therapy sessions turned into a passionate love affair. At first, it felt as if all my troubles had disappeared, but then Simone came to visit.

From the moment she landed in Cape Town until she left two weeks later, I ran around desperately trying to please three women. On her arrival, Simone laid down the rules: 'I've flown ten thousand kilometres to be with you. The least I expect is for you to be with me for the next two weeks.' Not to be outdone, Turcia made her demands too. 'I hope you're not hanging me out to dry?' In from the cold came Merilyn, who'd got wind that Simone was in town. She too asserted her claim. I was busted.

At the end of the two weeks, I'd failed miserably. Simone left Cape Town dejected. Merilyn discovered my affair with Turcia and was livid: 'You bastard! It's the second time you've done this to me.' For Turcia it was all too much: she put an end to our affair and resigned from Abrahams Kiewitz. For days, I moped in my apartment, feeling sorry for myself. I had no one but myself to blame. I'd been so engrossed in my own selfish world, doling out selective love, that I'd been oblivious to the real love and emotions that Merilyn, Simone and Turcia showed towards me. In a way, I was no different from my father; I had not physically abused my lovers, but I'd abused them emotionally. With Simone gone and Merilyn having ended what was left of our relationship, I vowed to make a fresh start: 'No more women in my life.'

However, a few days before Turcia was due to leave, she revealed that she was pregnant. The next few days were excruciating. Merilyn took the news in silence, but it clearly shook her. Next was Simone. With the bit of integrity left in me, I took the first available flight to Frankfurt. She was surprised at my unannounced visit, and thought I'd changed my mind and decided to move to Germany. When she learnt the real reason, she broke down and cried. 'I'd so much looked forward to a life with you. Now it's over,' she sobbed. We didn't speak for the rest of the evening. The following morning, I left quietly.

On 27 October 2001, in the early hours of a calm, beautiful spring morning, Turcia gave birth to a healthy baby boy. I couldn't hold back my emotions as I held him in my arms. Charles Junior, as we named him, ushered in a new era in my life.

24

Taking on Wall Street

Soothsayers are supposed to be able to predict the future. Some argued that the civilised world would be destroyed by the Y2K bug on 1 January 2000, when computer dates rolled over from '99' to '00' and the programs would supposedly function as if we had gone back to 1900. As scary as it sounded, I wish it had happened, as it would have wiped away billions of dollars of debt owed by poor southern countries to rich northern countries. Sadly, those debts remained.

In 1998, a global civil society movement named Jubilee 2000 made international headlines when more than one hundred thousand demonstrators gathered in Birmingham to present leaders of the G8 countries (the US, UK, Russia, Germany, France, Italy, Japan and Canada) with a petition, signed by over twenty-four million people around the world, demanding that the debt of the world's poorest countries be cancelled. One of its notable supporters, Pope John Paul II, used his moral authority to appeal for decisive steps towards resolving the global debt crisis. Jubilee 2000's moral call was based on the biblical jubilee, which was celebrated every fifty years. The land was supposed to lie fallow, debts were cancelled and slaves were set free.

My thesis attracted Jubilee's attention. They were interested in the legal arguments I'd made regarding apartheid's odious debts, and Jubilee South Africa, the movement's local chapter, invited me to address its annual conference on the findings of my research. For three years, it had mounted a spirited campaign, calling upon the post-apartheid democratic government to cancel the apartheid debts. 'South Africans shouldn't pay twice for their own oppression', read its popular slogan. My presentation landed me my first international law brief. I was asked to provide a legal opinion on how best to hold foreign banks and corporations accountable for supporting the apartheid regime.

After a few months of preparation, I presented my opinion to the leadership of Jubilee South Africa. Present at the meeting was seasoned human rights lawyer and trusted Jubilee patron Advocate Dumisa Ntsebeza. He'd served as a commissioner of South Africa's Truth and Reconciliation Commission (TRC), headed by Archbishop Desmond Tutu. Then there was Mallet Pumelele Giyose – or MP, as he preferred to be called – the organisation's newly elected chairperson. A large and imposing figure, he was an old anti-apartheid struggle stalwart who'd spent more than thirty years in exile. Despite having gradually lost his eyesight, his political astuteness indicated a crystal-clear vision. Dwarfed by MP was Neville Gabriel, the organisation's national administrator, who also represented the Catholic Church.

I began with a bold assertion: 'I don't think the government of South Africa has the political will to repudiate the apartheid debts.' I felt that the post-apartheid governments of presidents Nelson Mandela and Thabo Mbeki didn't want to upset the international financial markets, to whom the apartheid debts were due, and opted instead to pay.

I was unsure how my opinion would be received, but I got immediate support from MP and Dumisa. Neville took a contrary view. 'With dialogue and pressure, we can persuade the government to do the right thing,' he said.

After some fervent, snappy debate, I proceeded with my presentation. I'd come across a little-known law in the United States – the Alien Tort Statute (ATS) – which I believed was the key to holding foreign banks and corporations liable for supporting the apartheid regime. In short, the statute allowed non-US nationals to file civil suits in a United States district court against any person or corporation that had violated customary international law. After fielding a flurry of questions, I noticed MP nodding his approval. Everyone agreed that this was the way forward. As Jubilee South Africa was a coalition of many organisations, I proposed that the Khulumani Support Group take the lead. Khulumani had been established in the wake of the TRC and many of its members had testified before the TRC. My proposal was accepted.

There remained one troubling issue. A US lawyer named Edward Fagan had read about Jubilee South Africa's campaign against the apartheid debts and offered his services. But Fagan was a controversial figure. He came to prominence in the groundbreaking Holocaust class-action lawsuits filed against Swiss banks that had collaborated with the Nazis. The banks had retained and concealed assets of Holocaust victims and laundered the profits of slave labour. The lawsuits were settled for $1.25 billion, but Fagan was deemed an embarrassment to the legal profession for neglecting his clients while making millions in legal fees.

In September 2000, the *New York Times* ran an article in which it detailed a litany of client complaints against Fagan:

> As he recast himself as a 'human rights lawyer', Mr Fagan left neglected personal-injury clients in his wake, abandoning their claims or not returning their phone calls for years, according to court papers and interviews. One former client recently won a malpractice judgment against Mr Fagan and ethics officials in New Jersey filed a misconduct complaint against him last month on behalf of another client.

Unperturbed by these reports, Fagan had flown to Cape Town before Jubilee South Africa had even considered his offer. The leadership reluctantly agreed to meet with him, but no one offered a warm welcome. MP was furious that Fagan had placed an advert in a local newspaper that read like a poster from the Wild West: 'Wanted – Victims of Apartheid'. 'Bloody ambulance chaser!' lamented MP.

Fagan wasn't bothered by the frosty reception and cheerfully introduced himself. 'I'm Edward Fagan but you can call me Ed.'

Before he could get comfortable, MP had a go at him. 'How dare you come to this country and think you can solicit clients like they are cattle? It doesn't work like that. You must decide whether you're a law firm or a political organisation.'

The meeting went quiet. I thought Fagan would concede and apologise, but a war of words erupted instead. 'I resent your words, MP,' Fagan fired back. 'I've flown all the way to Cape Town, leaving behind other winnable cases in the US.' This was a reference to slave reparations cases. 'If Jubilee doesn't want to be involved with me, I have other South African clients I could turn to.'

Dumisa intervened and calmed the room. He proposed that Fagan be given a chance to state his case, but the air remained charged.

'The overall goal of the cases I'm involved in is to force settlements against large corporations,' Fagan said. 'For that to happen, Jubilee must move quickly, as there's a window of opportunity to pressurise banks and corporations into a settlement.'

I was surprised by the cavalier manner in which Fagan spoke of such an important issue. 'Don't you think you should provide us with a well-crafted legal plan before we move forward?' I asked. 'Can you at least provide us with a draft complaint?'

'Yes, I can,' he responded, 'provided Jubilee agrees to utilise my services.'

It was clear that Fagan intended to railroad Jubilee into a hasty decision. It infuriated me. The meeting eventually agreed that Jubilee South Africa would revert to him if it wanted to engage his services. I hoped that they wouldn't, but I knew it wouldn't be easy to get rid of Fagan. He wanted in on the case, badly.

A few months later, I got a call from Neville. His instructions were clear: 'Please assemble a team of international researchers and get us the best lawyer in the US. Not Ed Fagan, please.' I was relieved. I'd already contacted three renowned Swiss and German researchers: Mascha Madörin, Martina Egli and Gottfried Wellmer. They had authored a report titled 'The apartheid-caused debt: The role of German and Swiss finance', and readily agreed to my proposal. It didn't take me long to put the rest of the team together. All that remained was to find the right US lawyer. One name kept popping up across Switzerland, Germany and the US: Michael Hausfeld, one of the leading US lawyers in the Swiss Holocaust cases.

Hausfeld was highly regarded by his peers. The *National Law Journal* named him one of the top one hundred influential lawyers in America, while the *Global Competition Review* praised him for 'consistently bringing in the biggest judgments in the history of law' and being 'determined to change the world'. Not only did these tributes sway me, but like Kentridge and Platts-Mills, Hausfeld was definitely the kind of person from whom I could learn.

By the time I approached him, he'd already heard about our cause. 'I'd be happy to take on the case,' he said softly in a telephone call. 'Let me know when you and Jubilee are ready to meet.'

I was excited that my first international law case was finally coming to fruition, but life has a cunning way of tempering one's excitement, and it did so on 16 June 2002. It was a hot and humid day in Pietermaritzburg, where I was cheering on the Comrades Marathon runners. The runners epitomised true comradely spirit as they pulled each other along, some even helping one another to cross the finishing line.

Amid the camaraderie, I got an unexpected call from Glenda Loebell-Ryan, an old anti-apartheid activist living in Switzerland.

'Did you hear the news?' she asked, her voice frantic.

'What news?'

'It's all over the media,' she snapped. 'Ed Fagan has filed a class-action complaint on behalf of apartheid victims. He's in Zurich, parading Hector Pieterson's mother, Mrs Dorothy Molefi, on Paradeplatz in front of the cameras.'

I was shell-shocked. I couldn't utter a word.

'And guess with whom? Dumisa Ntsebeza.'

Right there, my world crumbled. I'd always had a hunch that Fagan would go it alone, but I had not thought that Dumisa would join him. Devastated, I promptly left the marathon and went back to my hotel. How could Dumisa do such a thing? Doubting Glenda's message, I decided to phone him and cut straight to the chase.

'Dumisa! Is it true?'

He took a deep breath, followed by a brief lull. Then he said, 'Charlie, my broe, I so much wanted to tell you beforehand. I never had the time to do so.' My heart sank. 'Jubilee took too long so I decided to go along with Ed. I did it for my younger brother, Lungisile.'

I'd held Dumisa in high regard for the outstanding work he'd done as a former TRC commissioner, but that day my regard for him took a beating.

'Why didn't you tell us? Why go with Fagan instead of waiting for Jubilee?'

But he was in no mood to respond. 'That's how it is, Charlie.' Our conversation ended on that bitter note.

By then the news had spread and my phone began to ring incessantly. MP was the first to call. 'Damn Dumisa! How could he do this to Jubilee?' he raged. Yasmin Sooka, a fellow Jubilee patron and former TRC commissioner, was equally dismayed. 'I'm truly shocked,' she said. Jubilee South Africa was thrown into a crisis. What next? It was an evening of great consternation and I felt as if my first international law case had gone up in smoke.

The following morning, I took an early flight to Cape Town. By then, the news was all over the country. 'Apartheid victims to sue top US and Swiss banks', read the *Business Day* headline. 'Maverick lawyer Ed Fagan is seeking as much as $50 billion for about eighty plaintiffs in South Africa.' Swiss newspapers featured sensationalist pictures in which Fagan appeared to be dragging Mrs Molefi past booing onlookers on Paradeplatz. His criticisms of the Swiss in the Holocaust cases and his self-serving, unprofessional conduct had earned him such a poor reputation that his apartheid class action now looked like another greedy attempt at exploiting traumatised victims for profit and status. It wasn't what I'd had in mind.

That day, Jubilee South Africa hurriedly released a press statement in an attempt at unity:

> This is a high point in a long battle we started more than three and a half years ago ... This international court action should therefore not come as a surprise ... Jubilee South Africa therefore calls on Swiss, American, German and British political and business leaders to convene an international conference with representatives of the banks, businesses, and civil society campaigning groups to decisively address this matter.

However, Dumisa had caused turmoil within the ranks of Jubilee South Africa and we were far from unified.

Back in Cape Town, I scheduled a teleconference with Michael Hausfeld for the following day. The news didn't surprise him. 'This is who Ed Fagan is,' he said. 'We should stick with our plan and file our own lawsuit.'

It had been an awful few days and the worst was about to come. I'd hardly put the phone down when a staff member screamed, 'Help! Help!' and six heavily armed gunmen stormed into my office, their weapons pointed at us.

'Where's the fucking money! Where's the fucking money! Tell us or we'll kill you all!' they shouted in broken English. Before I could respond, one of the gunmen pistol-whipped me. 'Don't talk! Just show us the fucking money.' I immediately obliged and led them to the safe. 'Hamba!' he shouted and pushed me away. They ransacked the safe, taking money, cameras, laptops and even a client's firearm. It was over as quickly as it had started, but it felt like an eternity. 'On the ground!' the others yelled. 'Close your eyes!' I feared the worst. *This is it! Today I'm going to die.* I'd survived gang fights and shootings right outside my door, and here I was, about to be shot by unknown tsotsis. I closed my eyes and waited for the gunfire. Everything went quiet.

After a while, I opened my eyes; the room was empty. Then the shock sank in. Our staff members Anthea and Tamzin were hysterical as we tried to reassure one another. It didn't take long for the police to arrive. As they combed the scene and took down statements, I drifted aimlessly, trying to make sense of what had happened.

The following day, the office opened as normal, leaving little time for any of us to deal with the shock. Some say this is how people cope with the trauma of violence in the new South Africa, but to me, that's how it has always been. The incident didn't dampen my resolve to continue with the litigation. On the contrary, I felt more determined to see it through. The senseless violence that had broken, maimed and destroyed lives under apartheid was not going to disappear simply because of the regime's official demise. We had every reason to hold accountable those who'd profited from apartheid while ordinary people were, and continue to be, subjected to this scourge.

—m—

On 11 November 2002, after months of intense legal research, we filed our class action complaint in a New York district court against twenty-three foreign multinational corporations and banks. The list of defendants read like the who's who of Wall Street: seven oil companies (ExxonMobil Corporation, Royal Dutch Shell, two Chevron oil companies, British Petroleum PLC, Total Fina Elf and Fluor Corporation, an engineering and construction company that diversified into oil and coal between the 1960s and 1980s); one arms company (Rheinmetall AG); eight banks (Barclays National Bank Ltd, Citigroup Inc., Commerzbank AG, Credit Suisse Group AG, Deutsche Bank AG, Dresdner Bank AG, JPMorgan Chase & Co. and UBS Group AG); three motor companies (Ford Motor Company, DaimlerChrysler AG and General Motors Company); three technology companies (Fujitsu Ltd, International Business Machines Corporation (IBM) and AEG Daimler-Benz Industrie); and one mining company (Rio Tinto Group).

They stood accused of aiding and abetting apartheid-sanctioned extrajudicial killings, rape, torture, arbitrary detention and inhumane treatment. Ninety-three members of the Khulumani Support Group recounted their ordeals to be documented in the legal complaint (summons). Among them was Thandiwe Shezi. She was twenty-six years old when, in 1988, about fifty soldiers and security policemen stormed into her Soweto home, looking for guns. When their search yielded nothing, police beat and strangled Shezi in front of her young daughter. They then bundled her into a car and drove her to a nearby police station.

The security police tied a sack over her head and poured water on it, followed by acid. The acid got into one of her eyes causing permanent damage to her eyesight. Thereafter, she was tortured with a stun gun for nearly half an hour.

Shezi was taken into a dark room where she was stripped and repeatedly raped by four police officers. 'We must just humiliate her and show her that this ANC can't do anything for her,' they said, according to her TRC testimony. 'If we do this humiliation act on her, she will speak the truth.'

After the gang rape, the police took Shezi to a doctor and told him that she was a prostitute who'd tried to flee when they wanted to arrest her. Shocked and terrified, she remained quiet. After the medical examination, she was taken to Diepkloof Prison, where she was placed in solitary confinement for about three months.

Then there was Anton Fransch (represented by his brother Mark Fransch), a trained operative of uMkhonto we Sizwe (MK, the armed wing of the ANC). On the morning of 17 November 1989, Fransch was accosted at his hideout in Athlone after being betrayed by a fellow operative who had been coerced into revealing the names of his comrades. The thirty-odd policemen and soldiers who came for him had no intention of taking him alive. 'Kom uit, jou vark! Vandag vrek jy!' they shouted. (Come out, you pig! You die today!) Armed with only a Makarov pistol and an AK-47, Fransch kept them at bay for seven hours, but eventually they overpowered and killed him.

In light of these testimonies, it is appalling that some defendants were proud of their association with the apartheid regime. For Barclays Bank, it was an honour to buy South African Defence Bonds, as its managing director, Bob Aldworth, proudly proclaimed in 1976: 'The bank regards the subscription as part of its social responsibility not only to the country at a particular stage in its history, but also to our staff members who have been called up [on national military service]'. Barclays Bank directors also served on the Defence Advisory Board.

Swiss firm Oerlikon Contraves and German firm Rheinmetall were two major arms suppliers to the apartheid regime during the 1970s and 1980s. Dieter Bührle of Oerlikon was the son of a German émigré, Emil Bührle, who'd become a Swiss national and had established the arms company, which became famous for its 20-mm anti-aircraft cannon. During the Second World War, his company sold the anti-aircraft cannon to both Nazi Germany and British Allied forces, making Emil Bührle, at one stage, the wealthiest man in Switzerland.

When he died in 1956, Dieter Bührle took over and became the darling of apartheid South Africa. His mission was to keep supplying arms and ammunition to South Africa, no matter the costs. In 1978, the apartheid government awarded him its highest military honour. German arms company Rheinmetall was no different. In 1979, it used a fake front company in Paraguay to export an entire ammunitions plant.

When the ship reached Brazil, it reloaded the ammunitions plant onto another ship destined for Durban. By 1985, at the height of civil unrest in South Africa, the Rheinmetall plant was fully operational. In 1999, it acquired Oerlikon Contraves and in 2008 it joined South African defence company Denel to form Rheinmetall Denel Munition.

The responses from some of the corporations were swift. Peter Wuffli, then chief executive officer of UBS bank, was quick to say, 'The business operations of UBS during the apartheid regime did not violate human rights', and the spokesperson for Credit Suisse argued, 'To give the Credit Suisse Group part of the responsibility for the injustices of apartheid is without basis and is not supported in any way by the facts.'

I'd had no illusions regarding their reactions; we were in for a massive fight.

25

Still waiting for the Big Apple

It's said that if you can't stand the heat, get out of the kitchen. By the time we'd filed the Khulumani complaint, the kitchen was already on fire. Fagan filed a series of further complaints, but even though he'd sullied the case, Hausfeld and I had no intention of leaving.

Our attempts at distinguishing the Khulumani lawsuit from Fagan's complaints ignited a bitter feud and brought me head-to-head with Dumisa Ntsebeza. Newspapers had a field day, with sensational headlines such as 'Rival reparations lawyers square off'. To make matters worse, the South African government opposed the litigation out of fear that it would drive investment away from South Africa. It filed a formal declaration in which it asked the court to dismiss the lawsuits. We didn't agree, as we believed that corporate accountability would attract rather than scare off investment.

Shirley Gunn, a founding member of Khulumani and former MK member, was outraged by the government's decision to oppose the lawsuits. 'First the government heaped scorn on the TRC recommendations by giving peanuts to the victims and now they want to take our rights away,' she said in a Khulumani meeting. 'This government is not serious about reparations.'

The defendant corporations seized the moment by portraying the litigation as nothing but an attempt at holding banks and corporations liable for merely doing business with apartheid South Africa, something, they asserted, that neither US foreign policy nor international law prohibited. Our response was simple: 'Khulumani's complaint is about the substantial assistance the defendants knowingly provided to the South African security apparatus that furthered the commission of gross human rights violations.' Even Archbishop Desmond Tutu and some of his former TRC commissioners supported the lawsuits by filing an amicus brief (a legal document from non-litigants with a strong interest in the case, offering advice for the court to consider):

> The decisions [to be] made by the court will shape the future of human rights litigation. They will reverberate beyond the courthouse walls to the ears of official and private actors across the globe. What happens to Khulumani matters not only to the victims of torture and murder who are plaintiffs in the case, it matters to victims worldwide.

—∿∿—

The hearing was scheduled for 6 October 2003 in the United States District Court for the Southern District of New York. It was my first trip to the city, and the weather was cold, wet and miserable. In the wake of 9/11 two years earlier, security at court was tight; demands for proof of personal identity and intrusive body searches marked the first obstacle to the case. As we got into a lift, a group of the defence lawyers joined us. No one spoke, and everyone stared straight ahead. The courtroom was full with the defendants' lawyers and what looked like their corporate clients. It felt like I'd walked into a corporate den, full of sleek men and women, well groomed and meticulously dressed.

As I surveyed the courtroom, I noticed Dumisa standing by himself. I walked over to him and we embraced each other, putting aside the acrimony between us.

'I'm glad you could make the trip,' he said.

'Likewise,' I responded. I dared not ask about Ed Fagan, who was conspicuously absent. In his place was another lawyer, Michael Osborne. It seemed the penny had dropped.

Soon, Judge John Sprizzo entered and proceedings began. He was short and stocky and gave the impression of being a no-nonsense type. Had it not been for his grumpy face, I would have mistaken him for actor Danny DeVito. There were legendary stories about Judge Sprizzo. In one, he'd let off a group of alleged heroin dealers and blamed his decision on an inept prosecution. 'You people have not been trained the way I have been trained,' he lambasted the prosecution. 'If you had been a competent prosecutor, which you are not, you would have hedged against the possibility that maybe the judge would disagree with you ... But even if I am wrong on the law, if they are walking out of here it is because you people were not competent enough to put in an extra charge in your indictment.' I couldn't tell whether this anecdote was a good or bad omen for our case, but it worried me.

The defendants presented their case first. Francis Barron, a senior litigation partner at Cravath, Swaine and Moore LLP, one of New York's premier law firms, proceeded straight to what was the cornerstone of the defendants' case – that commerce with apartheid South Africa was permitted and even encouraged. 'And, your Honour will recall, the United States adopted a policy of constructive engagement,' he submitted. 'That policy permitted and encouraged commercial interaction with South Africa on the theory that that was the way to bring about peaceful change.'

His submission didn't surprise me, but I was interested in Judge Sprizzo's response. At first, his face didn't reveal much, but it didn't take long for him to voice his views about arms sales to apartheid South Africa. 'I take it, whatever we were doing, other nations were selling them arms. South Africa was buying arms from other people. So was Iraq, which was embargoed.' He shrugged. 'I don't think anybody abides by those rules even if they are in effect because obviously there is a self-interest in selling your weapons wherever you can.'

My worries were aroused; Judge Sprizzo had expressed blatant disregard for international law. It seemed his mind had already been made up and he'd sided with the defendants. The rest of Barron's submissions went relatively well.

With Michael Osborne, Sprizzo was abrupt and abrasive, constantly interjecting. Osborne had hardly made his initial submissions before Sprizzo laid into him: 'If these corporations had not done business in South Africa and provided jobs for blacks even at reduced wages, as opposed to what many people may have been earning, they would have been unemployed altogether.'

'But our contention is different,' argued Osborne. 'The companies collaborated with the security forces; they aided and abetted the apartheid regime, and for this contention there is a lot of support in the decisions of the international criminal tribunals.'

Sprizzo scoffed at him. 'I'm not inclined to embrace the decisions of the International Court, especially when our government is refusing to be bound by decisions of the International Court in Brussels. Is that where it is? They want to try people for war crimes, etcetera. Haven't we refused, as a government, to be bound by those decisions?'

I shook my head in disbelief; at the very least I'd expected Sprizzo to know that the International Criminal Court was in The Hague in the Netherlands.

Next was our lawyer Michael Hausfeld. I had no reason to believe he could turn the tide, but his opening statement was unusual: 'If the Nazis had won World War II, would you say genocide is not a crime against humanity?' This got the court's attention.

There was a moment of suspense before Sprizzo responded. 'Probably. The Germans would define the rule. How can there be any law without the power to enforce it?'

Hausfeld quickly rebutted: 'I'm not sure, your Honour, that the oppressor sets the rules for what humanity otherwise condemns.'

Sprizzo and Hausfeld's scrimmage created a reflective moment in which two opposing legal camps were pitted against each other – international law with the authority to enforce it, and international law without that authority. I'd always thought that some legal principles were so firmly rooted in our moral fibre that their existence required no legal enforcement. The fact that powerful Western states had refused to declare apartheid a crime against humanity didn't mean apartheid wasn't a crime. But Judge Sprizzo was unconvinced by this argument and judgment was reserved.

—⁓—

A year later, on 29 November 2004, Judge Sprizzo delivered his judgment. Khulumani members had already prepared for the worst and, as expected, Sprizzo dismissed both the Khulumani and the Ntsebeza law-suits (named after Dumisa's younger brother). His ruling was a setback, but the claimants' spirits were not dampened. Maureen Mazibuko, who had been tortured by the South African police in 1977, was adamant that we keep going: 'No matter how long it takes, we must pursue these banks and companies and hold them liable for what they've done to the people of this country.' She wasn't alone in her resolve.

We promptly appealed Sprizzo's decision, and three years later, in 2007, the Second Circuit Court of Appeals overturned his decision. The ruling came as a welcome respite, but with a crippling caveat: the court held that corporate defendants could be held liable for civil pros-ecution, but only if the claimants showed that the corporations had intentionally aided and abetted crimes against international law.

'This is a death sentence,' said Hausfeld during a telephone call to me. 'Intention is a very high standard.' Given the secrecy in which the apartheid government conducted its business with foreign banks and corporations, we had little evidence to go by. It compelled us to drop the case against most defendants, leaving us with just eight: Barclays, Daimler, Ford, Fujitsu, General Motors, IBM, Rheinmetall and UBS. In 2009, the defendants made a failed bid for the Supreme Court to review the Appeals Court's decision, and the matter was sent back to the District Court, where it had started seven years earlier.

Sprizzo had died in 2008 and been replaced by Judge Shira Scheindlin, a breath of fresh air. She got proceedings under way and handed down her judgment two months later. She was meticulous in the way she crystallised the legal issues; from the types of torts that violated inter-national law to the relevant legal standard of aiding and abetting. Unfortunately, the prior Appeals Court decision had tied her hands, and she dismissed the claims against Barclays and UBS, leaving us to proceed only against Daimler, IBM, Ford, Fujitsu, Rheinmetall and General Motors.

It was like a rollercoaster. The remaining corporations showed no signs of letting up and promptly filed an appeal, which was heard a year later, in January 2010. On the upside, the mighty General Motors had filed for bankruptcy protection in 2009, and we doggedly pursued them in the bankruptcy court. In December 2011, General Motors settled and agreed to pay $1.5 million to the Khulumani and Ntsebeza claimants. It was a small amount, but a victory nonetheless. On the downside, we forwent the case against Fujitsu for lack of additional evidence to sustain our argument for aiding and abetting.

In 2013, three years after the appeal, judgment came in an unexpected form that sounded the death knell for the two cases. In a completely different matter (*Kiobel* vs *Royal Dutch Petroleum Co.*), the US Supreme Court held that the Alien Tort Statute did not apply to international law crimes committed outside the territory of the United States. In one stroke, the court had decided the fate of the Khulumani and Ntsebeza lawsuits, as most, if not all, of the international crimes took place in South Africa. Even though the writing had long been on the wall, I hadn't thought it would come to this, and despite a three-year flurry of further appeals, the US Supreme Court ended fourteen years of litigation on 20 June 2016.

The Khulumani members did not take the news well. Some said that the corporations had got away with murder. Others, such as Sakwe Balintulo, remained silent as I broke the news. Sakwe's brother Sabe was only fifteen years old when he was killed by police in 1973. Firebrand Maureen Mazibuko was not there for the defeat; she'd died in August 2012, after suffering multiple strokes.

My spirit was deflated; Wall Street had triumphed over justice. Only Shirley Gunn had comforting words: 'Don't despair. It's not over. We shall carry on fighting.'

26

We will not forgive them their trespasses

Despite the bruises it inflicted, the Khulumani litigation armed me with a powerful weapon – class-action lawsuits. Using these lawsuits, I had the ability to bring together hundreds, if not thousands, of people into a single case against one or more defendants, if they were affected by the same set of facts and laws. This was judicial efficiency at its best, and my intentions were firmly set on using class actions in South Africa, since very few poor and marginalised people could afford access to the courts. Unlike the United States and other countries, however, South Africa had no class-action laws. There was a 1998 draft class-action bill, but Parliament had yet to adopt it. I didn't plan to wait for Parliament to one day pass the law; I took the first available opportunity to undertake a class action in South Africa. That opportunity came in early January 2007, with news of a bread cartel.

Three of South Africa's largest bread-manufacturing companies – Pioneer Foods, Tiger Brands and Premier Foods – were all implicated in a decades-old bread cartel in which they had colluded to increase the price of bread. The news came as a shock to the country, as most of South Africa's poor and marginalised depended on bread as a daily staple.

It brought back painful memories of my own childhood, such as that day when I went without food and fought my dog Sheba for a few slices of stale, mouldy bread. 'Bastards! Fucking bastards!' I raged. 'How could they do this to poor people?' Despite my life having changed for the better, I felt compelled to do something.

The Competition Commission responded swiftly and embarked on a full-scale investigation. The saying 'There is no honour among thieves' held true, and Premier Foods was the first to break ranks and make a full disclosure to the commission. Tiger Brands followed shortly after with an agreement to pay the government a fine of R98 million. Pioneer denied all wrongdoing and put up a spirited fight before the Competition Tribunal (the adjudicatory body), but lost. It was ordered to pay R195 million in penalties. That would have been the end of it had it not been for my chance meeting with Imraahn Ismail Mukaddam.

Imraahn was a small-scale bread distributor from Elsies River who bought bread from Premier Foods and sold it to the public and other informal traders. It was the norm for him to receive a notice from Premier Foods informing him of the annual bread price increase. In December 2006, however, he got a telephone call from Premier Foods informing him that the three bread companies had met and agreed that each company would increase the price of its bread. Imraahn's instincts immediately kicked in. 'Something smelt fishy,' he said. 'It smelt like a cartel.' He promptly notified the Competition Commission.

As fate would have it, I received a call from my former supervisor, Steve Kahanovitz at the Legal Resources Centre, who asked that I assist Imraahn in an unrelated matter. I was only too happy to agree. After I'd dispensed with this other matter, I put the bread issue on the table. Imraahn was thrilled to hear that I was interested in his case, as he'd been looking for a lawyer to take on the bread companies for a long time. After blowing the whistle on the cartel, he found that no company would supply him with bread. Faced with the loss of his livelihood, he got desperate and sold his business to support his family.

'You need not look any further,' I assured him. 'You've found a lawyer.'

In the weeks that followed, I mapped out a broad legal strategy, and Imraahn convinced a number of small-scale bread distributors to join our case. I was determined to proceed by way of a class action, and all that remained was to put together a legal team. Ever since I'd stopped doing criminal work, I'd stepped back from court appearances, as I was more interested in making the cases happen while allowing others to argue them. I looked no further than my long-time colleague Advocate Renata Williams. She was eccentric and something of a maverick, with a cigarette permanently hanging from her lips. Her chambers were cluttered with documents and files. When I called her, she yelled, 'About bloody time someone did this! Yes, I'm taking the case.'

Renata and I agreed to proceed by way of two class actions – one on behalf of small-scale bread distributors, led by Imraahn, and the other on behalf of affected consumers, led by civil-society organisations (the Children's Resources Centre, the Black Sash, the Congress of South African Trade Unions and the National Consumer Forum). Because this was the first class action of its kind before a South African court, we had to be cautious and were required to approach the High Court for permission to proceed on a class-action basis.

The matter came before the Western Cape High Court on 24 September 2011. The courtroom was packed with members of the public, the media and lawyers. The bread companies had enlisted some of the country's top law firms – Edward Nathan Sonnenbergs (ENSafrica) for Tiger Brands; Cliffe Dekker Hofmeyr for Pioneer Foods; and Nortons Inc., a boutique law firm, for Premier Foods. Having grown accustomed to robust litigation, I was ready to face them. However, the matter got off to a rocky start. No sooner had Renata risen to present our case than Acting Judge Francois van Zyl interjected: 'I'm a bread consumer, too. Can I preside over this matter?'

There were audible gasps and laughter, but Renata responded quickly: 'Of course you can hear this case. As a judicial officer, you're excluded from the class.'

He seemed unconvinced, but allowed her to continue.

'By fixing the price of bread, the companies not only caused the consumers to pay more for bread; some poor consumers were unable to afford it. It violated their right of access to food,' she submitted.

The court listened attentively as Renata developed her legal arguments, but the judge soon intervened again. 'I'm concerned about the broadness of your case. I don't think every consumer's constitutional rights are affected. What about those consumers who can afford the increase in the price of bread? Certainly, their constitutional rights would not have been affected.' There were murmurs in court with nodding heads from the companies' lawyers.

'That may well be so,' Renata conceded, 'but the consumers' case is about the infringement of the constitutional right of *poor* consumers to have access to food. By unlawfully increasing the price of bread, the companies violated the right of poor consumers who had very little or no access to bread at all.'

She fielded a barrage of questions that continued for most of the day. Things didn't go as I'd hoped. In the afternoon, it was the companies' turn, and they pounced on every detail. Seasoned advocate Schalk Burger, representing Pioneer Foods, was forthright: 'There is no positive duty on the bread companies not to violate the right to food. That duty only pertains to the state.' He made his submissions with little interference from the judge. Advocate John Dickerson, representing Tiger Brands, tore through our submissions too. In the end, even I felt that our case for the constitutional right to food had been shredded. All that remained was for the Premier Foods advocate, Anton Katz, to finish the job the next day.

I knew Anton well as we'd worked together on other matters. He had no intention of letting up either and squarely directed his charge at me. 'There is a conflict of interest between the bread consumers and the small-scale bread distributors,' he submitted. 'The distributors would have passed on an increase in the price of bread to the consumers; Mr Abrahams can't act for both classes.' With this legal technicality, Anton had hammered the final nail into the coffin. Because the distributors had increased their prices in response to the bread companies, they too could be considered culpable in depriving the poor of their access to food. Anton's point was that the consumers' case was not really against the bread companies, but against the distributors, at least in legal terms. In addition, the distributors had not suffered a lack of access to food as poorer consumers had. Overall, this meant that I had made an error in representing them both. After two days of intense legal arguments, judgment was reserved for the following morning.

The next day, I wearily entered the courtroom. I hadn't slept in days and felt as if I'd been flattened by a bulldozer. Thankfully, proceedings moved quickly. The judge swept in and delivered a swift judgment. 'The cases involve difficult questions of law and try to break new legal grounds. However, given the time, it was impossible to write a judgment,' he said. 'The case of the consumers is dismissed with no order as to costs. The case of the small-scale bread distributors is dismissed with costs.' The court rose. It was all over, and the bread distributors had been ordered to pay the legal costs of the companies we'd tried to sue. Defeated, I remained seated and took a deep breath. The companies' lawyers were jubilant; my clients were speechless.

As the courtroom emptied, a journalist approached me. 'Is this the end of the road for the class actions, or are you going to appeal?'

I pulled myself together and put on a brave face. 'This matter is of huge public importance. Once we've received the full judgment, we'll consider our options.' But despite my response, I was ravaged.

My clients accompanied me to a nearby coffee shop. The mood was mixed. Marcus Solomon of the Children's Resources Centre struck a defiant note. 'If the bread companies think we're going to roll over and lie down, then they're making a big mistake. This is but the beginning.' He hadn't lost the defiant spirit he'd shown back in his days as a political prisoner on Robben Island. The others agreed.

Imraahn, however, did not take the judgment well. He had convinced the other bread distributors to join the lawsuit and felt responsible for the legal costs they now had to pay. 'First, I lost my business, and now there's a costs order against us,' he said, dejected.

'Don't worry,' I told him. 'We'll appeal the decision, even if it means going to the Constitutional Court.'

No sooner was the hype over than we launched our appeal. Given the onslaught we'd faced from the companies' lawyers, Renata and I agreed to enlarge our legal team. Wim Trengove, one of South Africa's most experienced and formidable legal minds, agreed to come on board. So, too, did others. Given Premier's argument that I had a conflict of interest and could not represent both classes, I approached Terence Matzdorff of Knowles Husain Lindsay and semi-retired advocate Paul Hoffman to act for the small-scale distributors. They kindly agreed.

The matter of whether or not we could proceed via class action came before the Supreme Court of Appeal in Bloemfontein a few months later, on 7 November 2012. The morning's gentle spring breeze could be considered a precursor to the legal history about to unfold. This time, the issues were crisp and the arguments much more refined. We made much of the argument that access to justice is a constitutional right, and class actions give access to those who cannot pursue justice on their own. The companies' lawyers, in turn, attempted to get the case dismissed by asserting that Parliament should lay down the law for class actions, not the courts. After two days of complex legal arguments, judgment was reserved, but then delivered a mere three weeks later.

I was in the office when the fax arrived. I stared at my secretary for a moment after she handed it to me, then turned toward my window. It overlooked a tranquil waterfall in Bellville, where we'd moved a few years earlier; a step up from our modest offices in Nooitgedacht.

When I paged through the judgment, I lit up. 'The appeal against the refusal to certify a class action,' it read, 'is upheld and the application is remitted to the High Court for determination in accordance with the principles in this judgment.' With those few gratifying lines, I knew we'd made legal history. We had made class-action procedures a feature of South African law.

The appeal court dismissed the companies' arguments that courts should wait for Parliament to enact class-action legislation. Instead, it provided guidelines to the High Court on how to certify class actions. I knew we'd have no difficulty complying with those guidelines and have our class action certified. Word spread quickly in the office and other lawyers and staff gathered to congratulate me.

Sadly, there was bad news too: the court had dismissed the case of the small-scale bread distributors, as it found no evidence that the bread prices would have been lower but for the unlawful conduct of the companies. On the bright side, Imraahn and the other small-scale distributors didn't have to pay the companies' legal costs. Buoyed by our success with the consumers' case, Hoffman and Matzdorff soldiered on to the Constitutional Court, as they believed that the small-scale distributors' constitutional rights to trade were infringed. Months later the court overturned the decision of the Supreme Court of Appeal and referred the matter back to the High Court to be assessed according to the class-action guidelines.

With two judgments in our favour, the tide had turned against the bread companies. Faced with the prospect of further litigation, they did not wait to see if we would be granted permission to file a class action. Instead, the companies reached confidential settlements with both the small-scale bread distributors and the civil-society organisations acting on behalf of the bread consumers.

This represented more than a professional victory for me. It was deeply personal. My childhood struggle for bread had not been in vain.

27

Arms before Azania

During the sixteenth century, a fabled city of gold known as El Dorado evoked images of such opulence and grandeur that the monarchs of Spain and England backed thousands of men in expensive expeditions to find it. They never did. At the same time, about eleven thousand kilometres away on the east coast of Africa, was a mythical utopia called Azania where high culture and vibrant commerce flourished. Tales about it exist to this day. For many, Azania evoked images of a place of milk and honey, and many, like me, believed that post-apartheid South Africa would be a new Azania. The euphoria of 1994 ushered in that prospect. Yet, at that very moment of liberation, sinister forces were already hard at work to scupper our dreams.

By the time South Africa had held its first democratic election, foreign navies, heads of state, arms dealers and middlemen from Britain, France, Germany and other Western countries had begun lining up to showcase their military hardware to Nelson Mandela's young government. Rumour had it that when Queen Elizabeth II visited South Africa in 1995, the royal yacht doubled as a floating arms exhibition. The arms dealers had a simple message: a prosperous South Africa deserved the best weapons.

It worked. Four years later, in December 1999, South Africa concluded an exorbitant arms package totalling just under R30 billion. Some R12.2 billion was spent on German corvette warships and submarines, R15.7 billion went to British Aerospace and SAAB for Gripen and Hawk fighter aircrafts, and a further R1.9 billion went to Italy for light utility helicopters. Not even the Reconstruction and Development Programme (RDP), adopted by the ANC-led government in 1994 as its main policy framework to reconstruct and develop a post-apartheid South Africa, had enjoyed such speedy financing. Hardly two years later, the government had all but abandoned the RDP in favour of yet another policy framework, Growth, Employment and Redistribution (GEAR). Even though it still espoused the goals of the RDP, the new policy focused on fiscal prudence, which meant reining in government spending. This didn't stop the government from incurring massive debt and spending it on arms.

Thus, South Africa joined a long list of young democracies and post-conflict countries that were hoodwinked into buying military hardware from international armament corporations working in concert with their respective Western governments. The bait dangled before our decision-makers was alluring: there would be countertrade worth R104 billion and the creation of 65 000 jobs. But very few, if any, of those jobs materialised.

It boggled my mind that the ANC-led government was so easily seduced into procuring arms. Their error reminded me of the biblical Esau, who sold his birthright (being the first-born son) to his twin brother Jacob for a pot of stew. In our case, it was more like we had given up our daily bread in exchange for arms.

It wasn't long after the conclusion of the Arms Deal that I attended an odious-debt conference in Bonn, Germany. During a break I was approached by a concerned young man from Nigeria. 'Do you South Africans know what you're getting yourselves into with your Arms Deal?' he asked. Before I could respond he added, 'Just look at Nigeria and see what misery our arms deals have brought us.' This young man was sounding a warning to the youngest of Africa's democracies, and his anguish still haunts me.

Three years later, in June 2003, I received an unexpected call from Terry Crawford-Browne, an anti–Arms Deal crusader. I'd met him at a Jubilee South Africa conference where I'd presented my research into apartheid's odious debts, and we'd spoken about the Arms Deal and its financial consequences for South Africa.

Terry had started legal proceedings against the South African government to have the Arms Deal cancelled, but he wasn't happy with the manner in which his legal team had conducted the case. 'I've sacked my legal team and need a lawyer. Can you represent me?' he said on the phone.

His request surprised me. At the time, I was fully occupied with the Khulumani class action in New York and barely had the ability to take on another big case. But I did not want to say no. The Arms Deal was the single largest foreign-debt transaction of the post-apartheid government. It may not have been an odious debt, but the need for an arms deal had always been questionable, as was our capacity to afford it. I decided to take it on.

Terry had already set his legal strategy in motion. He intended to have the loan agreements that financed the Arms Deal cancelled by the court, in the hope that this would collapse the deal. I expressed some reservations: it was a risky strategy as he wasn't seeking to cancel the military hardware agreements too. It was like trying to return a car purchased on credit. Two separate transactions have been combined into one, and you can't cancel the credit or loan agreement hoping that the agreement to purchase the vehicle automatically disappears too. You have to cancel both. Terry's one-legged strategy steered him on a direct collision course with minister of finance Trevor Manuel, who'd negotiated and entered into the loan agreements on behalf of the South African government.

Tempers flared, with Terry allegedly having called the minister a prostitute for signing the loan agreements, and the minister retaliating by calling Terry the gorilla on his back.

I tried to convince Terry that he needed to add the military hardware agreements to his case, because getting both agreements cancelled would give him a better chance at success. But Terry wouldn't budge. 'It's unnecessary,' he protested. 'Anyway, it would drag the case out for too long.'

Colleagues had warned me of Terry's stubbornness, a trait he blamed on his Irish blood. Once he'd made up his mind, that was it. This didn't ruffle me; I understood his impatience. By the time I got involved, Terry had already invested four years and most of his and his wife's life savings in the case. I chose to continue pursuing the matter, as its public interest far outweighed the difficulties caused by Terry's stubbornness.

The financial documents Terry obtained from the minister regarding the purchase of the arms made for compelling reading, exposing the dire financial consequences South Africans would face over the next twenty years. Because the Arms Deal was concluded in foreign currency, the R30-billion price tag was based on an exchange rate of R6.25 for each dollar. The slightest depreciation in the value of the rand would therefore increase the purchase price.

My fears of a debt trap were confirmed. The finance minister's own department expressed its concern that South Africa's growth rate would drop as the level of expenditure and repayments on the arms rose over a period of twenty years. The same would be true for increases in the interest rate.

A report from London-based consultancy Warburg Dillon Read concluded that not only would the financing of the Arms Deal add about 7 per cent to the national debt, but for every rand of depreciation in the dollar–rand exchange rate, the financing costs would increase the total foreign debt service by R2.5 billion and principal repayments by R4.8 billion.

In time, however, the cost of the Arms Deal was overshadowed by allegations of corruption, notably against then deputy president Jacob Zuma and his former financial advisor, Schabir Shaik – the latter having solicited a bribe on behalf of the former from a French arms company connected to the Arms Deal.

On 17 February 2004, the matter came before the Western Cape High Court. Because Terry had sacked his former legal team, few advocates were prepared to act for him. Fortunately, Advocate John van der Berg and his colleague Paul Eia agreed to argue the matter.

Van der Berg made much of the warnings by the experts, stating that these should have placed the minister on notice not to enter into and sign the loan agreements. 'The warnings were such that no rational person, acting rationally, could have ignored them in deciding whether to enter into the loan agreements,' he submitted.

But Advocate Michael Kuper, acting for the minister of finance, disagreed. He was emphatic that Terry had attacked the wrong decision; he should have attacked the government's decision to acquire the armaments. 'By the time the loan agreements were concluded, the cabinet decision was a fait accompli,' Kuper held. 'The minister's role was merely limited to that of finding the necessary funding in order to finance the acquisition.'

Kuper confirmed the concern I'd expressed about Terry's one-legged strategy, and the judges' comments heightened it. They reserved judgment.

In his book, *Eye on the Money*, Terry describes the morning of the judgment (4 March 2004) as cloudless and windless, but when I stepped into the courtroom the atmosphere was tense. Terry sat behind me as we waited for Judge André Blignault and Judge James Yekiso. Their judgment was as quick as their entry.

'Applicants' review application is dismissed with costs,' Judge Blignault read.

Gasps and sighs followed. Terry was stone-faced; he had, indeed, attacked the wrong decision, and the court had sided with the minister. 'The applicant's attack should have focused on the real and effective decision to acquire these arms, namely that of cabinet,' the court held.

It was a bitter pill for Terry to swallow, and to add to that he'd been slapped with the state's legal costs, amounting to more than one million rand. I, too, was gutted. I'd quietly held out the hope that the court would decide in Terry's favour, out of concern for the consequences that the increased foreign debt would have on the lives of ordinary South Africans. Money, I believe, that could have been put to better use in South Africa.

—⚏—

Terry was no ordinary client. Both he and his cases challenged political power in the face of ridicule and isolation – experiences I knew all too well. And the very source of Terry's weakness nevertheless proved to be the source of his strength: his stubbornness eventually pulled him through. A few years later, the state issued a formal application to have him sequestrated, while Trevor Manuel issued an interdict to prevent him from uttering certain statements against him. Even this did not stop Terry in his quest to have the Arms Deal cancelled, and I promised to assist him wherever I could. By August 2010, we were hard at work preparing another court challenge.

This time, Terry had convinced semi-retired advocates Paul Hoffman and Peter Hazell to come on board, and we used a different strategy. Instead of challenging the loan agreements, we would approach the Constitutional Court to compel President Jacob Zuma to appoint a commission of inquiry into the Arms Deal, based on the huge number of corruption allegations that had since been brought to public attention. Among the allegations were that British BAE Systems paid R1.7 billion in bribes to secure the lion's share of the Arms Deal; the German Frigate Consortium paid R130 million under the table to secure the corvettes; German MAN Ferrostaal's R30 million bribes went to secure the submarine contracts; and R24 million was paid out surreptitiously by the Swedish SAAB subsidiary. I hoped a commission would confirm these corruption allegations and get the Arms Deal cancelled.

The years since his bruising encounter with Trevor Manuel had moderated Terry's temperament, and he was happy with our legal strategy. It was an extraordinary step, as direct access to the Constitutional Court is only granted in exceptional circumstances, if the interests of justice dictate it. We had good reason. President Jacob Zuma had failed to appoint an independent commission of inquiry despite numerous requests by Terry and other eminent South Africans. Only the Constitutional Court could compel him to do so.

The president opposed the application, and his lawyers portrayed Terry as an annoying litigant, pointing to his string of failed cases and unpaid legal bills.

At the Constitutional Court in Braamfontein on the morning of 5 May 2011, the customary introductions went smoothly, but Chief Justice Sandile Ngcobo stopped Advocate Hoffman before he could make his submissions. Addressing both Hoffman and Advocate Marumo Moerane, the president's counsel, Ngcobo said that the court was ready to proceed, but that proceedings would be hampered without the president's full version before court. Moerane was faced with a dilemma: either he proceeded with his technical arguments or he opted for a postponement to add more facts to the president's papers. He went with the latter.

The court granted both parties an opportunity to supplement their papers and postponed the matter to 20 September 2011 – a rather flat note on which to end the day after so much anticipation. And that was where the matter ended, full stop. We would not step into the Constitutional Court to argue this matter again.

On 12 September 2011, the wily President Zuma agreed to establish a commission of inquiry into the Arms Deal. It was surreal; none of us had expected it to come this quickly, or in the manner that it did. After so many weary years of litigation, there was no excitement, and Terry took the news in his stride when I broke it to him. I guess the relentless perseverance had numbed him. Or perhaps he knew what lay ahead.

The commission was a huge disappointment. It took more than four years, only to find that, despite overwhelming evidence, there had been no undue influence or evidence of corruption in the selection of the preferred bidders. The commission's findings were a slap in the face for Terry. Critics dismissed the findings as a whitewash.

Whatever the merits or demerits of the commission's work, South Africa's foreign debt had increased from about R100 billion in 1994 to R2.6 trillion in 2018; economic growth had decreased and the rand had lost more than half its value. The cost of the Arms Deal has substantially increased, some suggesting figures between R70 billion and R90 billion. Yet, despite the staggering costs, I am not aware of any former minister, president or senior official publicly acknowledging that the Arms Deal was one of the government's biggest post-apartheid mistakes – if not *the* biggest – and apologising for it. To this day, there remains a deafening silence.

Whenever I think back to that conference in Bonn, I remember the concern I saw in the eyes of that young Nigerian. Not only did we fail ourselves, we failed our fellow Africans. We have been unable to rise to the challenge so eloquently expressed by Nelson Mandela in his inaugural speech in 1994: 'Let there be work, bread, water and salt for all.' The opportunity to create Azania has been squandered, and it remains as far out of our reach as El Dorado.

28

All that is gold does not glitter

'All that is gold does not glitter,' wrote J.R.R. Tolkien in *The Lord of the Rings*, suggesting that the great value we find in gold comes in more than one form. Other things, like human resilience in the face of drudgery, are treasures too.

By the time *The Fellowship of the Ring* was published in 1954, gold had been integral to South Africa's economic life for almost seven decades. Discovered in 1886 on the Witwatersrand (some four hundred kilometres from where Tolkien was born in 1892 in Bloemfontein), gold gave added prominence to the name of the diamond man Cecil John Rhodes.

Rhodes was a quintessential British imperialist. His infamous essay 'Confession of Faith' sets out his grandiose vision of a British Empire:

> I contend that we are the finest race in the world and that the more of the world we inhabit the better it is for the human race. Just fancy those parts that are at present inhabited by the most despicable specimens of human beings, what an alteration there would be if they were brought under Anglo-Saxon influence, look again at the extra employment a new country added to our dominions gives.

Rhodes devotes the remainder of 'Confession of Faith' to the establishment of a secret society that would achieve his ultimate goal. He fails, however, to describe the kind of 'alteration' that would result if those 'despicable specimens' were brought under Anglo-Saxon influence. Through his legacy, a grim picture of death and destruction emerged.

In 1887, Rhodes and his associate Charles Rudd formed the company Gold Fields of South Africa. Forty years later, Gold Fields, together with the rest of South Africa's gold-mining industry, employed about a quarter of a million miners. In the decades that followed, that number grew to half a million men. The gold-mining industry showed an endless thirst for Rhodes's 'despicable specimens' as it transformed South Africa's rural economy into a modern industrial one.

When South Africa's exploitation of cheap black labour began in earnest, tens of thousands of young black men were uprooted from rural areas and transported wholesale, like cattle, to the gold mines in Johannesburg and the Free State. Alfred Temba Qabula, a writer and trade unionist whose father was a migrant labourer, portrays this deception and displacement in his poem 'The Small Gateway to Heaven':

> When the recruiters invaded our homes
> to get us to work the mines
> They would say:
> 'Come to Malamulela
> at Mlamlankuzi with its hills and valleys
> There are mountains of meat
> There a man's teeth become loose from endless chewing
> And there where the walls are grumbling
> Where the stoneface is singing
> Promising bridewealth and merriment
> Where sorrows disappear at the wink of an eye
> Come to the place of the
> Hairy-jaw
> where starvation is not known.'
>
> And we joined the queues through the small gate to Heaven.
> And we found the walls of our custody
> and degradation
> and of work darkness to darkness
> with heavy shoes burdening our feet
> with worry

For nothing
At the place of the Hairy-jaw
away from our loved ones

And I have seen this prison of a Heaven
This kraal which encircles the slaves

And I saw it as the heart of our oppression
And I saw the walls that separate us
from a life of love.

—◊—

Fast-forward a century, to when Richard Spoor and I became determined to address one of the consequences of this atrocity – occupational lung diseases. I had met Richard at a civil-society conference in Johannesburg in 2003. He was already well known as an occupational-lung-disease lawyer, his latest success being a major settlement for miners with asbestosis. These miners had worked at Gencor mines, once one of South Africa's largest mining houses. We immediately found common ground.

Richard was impressed with my class action in the United States and our conversation soon turned to the topic of gold. 'I've been eyeing the gold-mining industry for a while,' he said. 'So what do you say about us teaming up against them? You with your class-action experience and me with my occupational-lung-disease experience?'

His invitation required no further consideration, and I promptly agreed. Occupational lung diseases such as silicosis and tuberculosis were rampant among gold-mine workers in South Africa. Silicosis, commonly known as miners phthisis, is contracted in dusty environments where workers inhale the fine silica dust particles created by activities such as the drilling, cutting or chipping of gold-bearing silica rocks. The silica particles cause scarring of the miners' lung tissue, making it difficult for them to breathe. Tuberculosis is a contagious airborne disease caused by bacteria. The large numbers of miners working together in dusty conditions provided the perfect breeding grounds for tuberculosis.

Between deciding to sue and the eventual class action, we were faced with a seemingly insurmountable legal hurdle: a long-held assumption that South Africa's mining industry was immune to legal suit. Mining companies paid a risk levy (also known as a dust levy) to a state compensation fund and argued that once a miner contracted silicosis or tuberculosis, his claim lay not against the mining company, but against the compensation fund. Richard and I considered this a legal fallacy that could not withstand a miner's constitutional and other rights to be free from harm caused by a mining company. Whether or not a miner had a claim against the compensation fund, we didn't think it absolved the mining companies of civil liability.

We decided to begin with a test case, and set off for Mthatha in the Eastern Cape, the heartland of former gold-mine workers. We met with miners who'd long wanted to pursue their claims and, after listening to us, they all wanted to be part of the test case. The responsibility for selecting a test claimant fell to me. A few weeks later, I chose Thembekile Mankayi, who had worked as an underground miner for AngloGold Ashanti (formerly Vaal Reefs Exploration and Mining Company Ltd) from 1979 to 1995. During this time, he'd contracted silicosis and his employment had been medically terminated. Mankayi was the ideal test claimant because he'd only worked for one company, and could therefore only have contracted silicosis in their mines. This meant that we could keep things relatively simple by suing only one defendant, instead of having to take on multiple defendants who could each deny being the cause of Mankayi's illness. Though only forty-eight years old, he looked as if the underground rock had been permanently etched into his face. The rest of his body was skin and bone. He eagerly agreed to take the lead.

US lawyer Michael Hausfeld, with whom I'd struck up a relationship during the Khulumani class action, agreed to finance the case. After months of careful consideration, we issued summons against AngloGold Ashanti in 2006 for R2.6 million in damages for having negligently exposed Mankayi to a dusty environment, resulting in his silicosis. As expected, AngloGold Ashanti opposed the action and made the point that Mankayi had no legal basis for his civil suit, as his only claim was against the compensation fund, not the company.

Richard and I were so convinced of the imminent success of our constitutional defence that, even before the matter came before Judge Meyer Joffe in the High Court in February 2009, we'd already made plans to track down thousands of former gold-mine workers. But to our surprise, Judge Joffe was not persuaded, and a few months later he upheld AngloGold Ashanti's submission that we had no legal basis on which to sue the company. It was a setback, but we were unperturbed and chose to appeal the ruling. A year later, the matter came before the Supreme Court of Appeal. With a bench of five judges, we thought we'd have better luck, but hardly had our advocate Gilbert Marcus got up to make his submissions, than he was bombarded with questions from all directions.

'Show us the provisions in ODIMWA, the Act you rely on,' one of the judges demanded, referring to the Occupational Diseases in Mines and Works Act. I pitied Marcus as he dodged bullets, trying to convince the judges of our case. Eventually, he gave up. Advocate Chris Loxton for AngloGold Ashanti had a smooth ride, and a few weeks later on 31 March 2010, all five judges ruled against Mankayi – a knockout blow. Our optimism took a serious beating and even our advocates gave up hope.

By then, we'd run out of money and the legal bills had piled up. To compound our problems, one of our advocates couldn't wait for overdue payments and decided to blacklist me, as I was in charge of finances. Summons followed shortly afterwards. Blacklisting notifies fellow advocates of delinquent lawyers who are unable to settle their bills on time. The advocate was within his rights to take this measure, but it came at the wrong time – both Richard and I were broke.

We were faced with a stark choice – call it quits or soldier on to the Constitutional Court. We chose the latter. As the more experienced lawyer, Richard agreed to argue the case himself, and the matter was set for 17 August 2010. Still reeling from my financial woes, I was unable to travel to Johannesburg on the day, but Richard called to report that he thought the arguments had gone rather well. For the first time in a long while, I felt a renewed sense of optimism.

Seven months later, on 3 March 2011, came the news I'd been waiting for: in a unanimous judgment, the Constitutional Court overturned the appeal court's judgment and ruled in favour of Thembekile Mankayi. It made five years of legal hardship all worthwhile. Judge Sisi Khampepe foreshadowed my lack of words when she quoted T.S. Eliot's poem 'Burnt Norton' in her judgment document:

> Words strain,
> Crack and sometimes break, under the burden,
> Under the tension, slip, slide, perish,
> Decay with imprecision, will not stay in place,
> Will not stay still

The judgment was a major victory for the tens of thousands of current and former gold-mine workers who could now file claims against gold-mining companies. The scene had been set for the largest legal battle in South African history. Unfortunately for Mankayi, the judgment came too late: he had died a week earlier. More than ever, Richard and I were determined to push ahead.

29

A taste of the mountains of meat

Undertaking a class action against South Africa's gold-mining industry was a colossal task that required deep pockets, which neither Richard nor I had. We had Hausfeld's backing, but Richard felt it wasn't enough. He approached Motley Rice, a large US law firm known for getting a settlement of $246 billion in its historic tobacco-industry class action. Motley Rice agreed to get involved, but wanted to finance the case and provide legal advice without Hausfeld. I vehemently disagreed and refused to abandon Hausfeld as a matter of loyalty and principle. Efforts to bring the two together failed, setting Richard and me on separate paths; something I hadn't thought possible months earlier.

On 21 August 2012, I fired the first volley: three class actions against AngloGold Ashanti, Gold Fields Limited and Harmony Gold. Four months later, in December 2012, Richard followed with his class action against the majority of the gold-mining industry, including the likes of Anglo American South Africa, African Rainbow Minerals and Sibanye Gold. Together, we were suing more than thirty South African gold-mining companies.

In response, the gold-mining industry marshalled the best of South Africa's law firms – Webber Wentzel for Anglo American; ENSafrica for AngloGold Ashanti; Cliffe Dekker Hofmeyr for African Rainbow Minerals; Norton Rose Fulbright for Gold Fields; and Hogan Lovells for Harmony Gold. These were no ordinary law firms; their global foot-print was extensive. Some scholars refer to them as the handmaidens of globalisation – the firms that wove the tapestry of global law. To square up against them was not easy.

A confluence of events counted in our favour. The world of Cecil

John Rhodes was no more and in its place was a democratic South Africa with a constitution that finally gave voice to millions of 'despicable specimens'. It was estimated that there were between eight hundred thousand and just over a million former gold miners scattered across southern Africa, a third of whom had been diagnosed with silicosis. Worse still were those suffering from tuberculosis, estimated to be at least three times more than those suffering from silicosis.

Once the enormity of the cases became apparent, Richard and I realised we needed each other. We made amends and agreed to consolidate our separate cases. Motley Rice and Hausfeld also agreed to cooperate. By then the Legal Resources Centre had joined the fray and together we formed a united front against the gold-mining companies. The next step was to acquire permission to proceed via class action, and the hearing was set for 12 to 23 October 2015.

—⚹—

Courtroom GC in the South Gauteng High Court was packed. Leading our joint teams was Advocate Wim Trengove, a trusted hand from the days of the bread-cartel class action. 'The mining companies failed to protect the workers against excessive levels of dust,' Trengove said in his opening submissions, 'and they failed to do so not out of ignorance, but because protection cost more than the statutory compensation they were required to pay. They had a powerful commercial incentive to neglect the health and safety of their workers, because it was cheaper to pay statutory compensation to diseased workers than it was to install proper safety measures, including ventilation.'

For three days, Trengove and our other advocates methodically argued for the miners' right to claim damages from the gold-mining companies, their right to access their claims through a court of law, and for the court to permit them to do so through a class action.

'The prima facie evidence shows that as a result of the high dust levels, the incidence of silicosis and tuberculosis was much higher than they should have been,' Trengove submitted. I listened pensively. The high levels of dust alone were not enough to sustain our case for tuberculosis. Whereas silicosis can only be caused by exposure to the silica particles in rock, tuberculosis can be contracted anywhere. But Trengove seemed to have it under control, and put it to the court that working underground in an excessively dusty environment was more likely to give a miner tuberculosis than not working in that environment. If so, then miners with tuberculosis also had a claim against the gold-mining companies. I found these submissions reassuring.

After three days of intricate legal arguments, it was the defendants' opportunity to argue against us. Leading the charge was Advocate Chris Loxton for AngloGold Ashanti, who had acted for the same company in the Mankayi matter. Loxton argued that there was a difficulty with the class action, and expressed concern about when the mining companies became aware that silica dust caused silicosis. He compared our case with a tobacco class action: 'In the case of a smoking class action, it starts with the tobacco companies being aware that smoking causes cancer, and stops when the public becomes aware thereof. Not so with this case.' His submissions irritated me, as the mining companies knew long ago that exposure to excessive silica dust causes silicosis.

Loxton and his colleagues proceeded to devote the better part of their arguments to the nuts and bolts of class actions: commonality (they didn't think that the conditions and circumstances of gold miners were the same across the gold mines in South Africa); suitability (they didn't think that a class action was the best method for the case even though they failed to put forward an alternative); and manageability (whether the court could manage such a large case).

The arguments were technical and at times wearisome, and I couldn't wait for Gold Fields' Jeremy Gauntlett to take the floor. Gauntlett was one of the finest legal minds the country had produced and for that he was either well liked or greatly disliked.

He wasted no time in his opening remarks: 'We adopt the position that this application for certification will lead to the creation of worse than a bus on square wheels.' For more than two days, Gauntlett and his colleague tenaciously explored each and every conceivable reason why the court should not certify the class action. The case for tuberculosis took a particular beating. 'The evidence is flimsy as to the connection between overexposure to silica dust and tuberculosis,' his colleague argued. 'The plaintiffs are relying on unreliable evidence.'

Meanwhile, a quiet storm was brewing. Richard had photographed one of the defendants' advocates apparently sleeping in court, and posted it on Facebook. His attempt to undermine the opposition backfired, badly. They were so angry at his unprofessional conduct that they brought it to the court's attention. Richard unreservedly apologised, but this was but a precursor to an even bigger controversy that threatened to overshadow the entire case.

A few days later, a colleague in the legal profession posted a Facebook comment about the fact that most of the lawyers involved in the case were white. The need for racial transformation in the legal sector is an important issue, as it is in most South African industries, but her statement lit Richard's fire. '[W]hy no black counsel [advocates] on my team?' he fired back. 'Reason number one is I use counsel who are willing to do work on a reduced fee ... Second we brief only exceptional counsel ... The number of black counsel who meet both these criteria are really small.' And if that wasn't enough, he added, 'The work I do doesn't leave much room for charity or experimentation.'

A full-blown social media storm erupted and the favourable news coverage that the case had enjoyed soured as journalists turned on Richard. 'Lawyer's charity jibe sparks race standoff' read the *Sunday Times*, followed by the *City Press* headline 'Wake-up call for black lawyers'.

That evening, I received a text from my long-time colleague Dumisa Ntsebeza, with whom I'd had a turbulent relationship during the Khulumani litigation. His text was forthright: 'Are you going to do anything about the most racist and patronising statement that Richard issued, denigrating black counsel? I would expect you to publicly distance yourself from that statement, condemning Spoor for saying those rabidly racist statements, unless of course you think the same way yourself – which I have no reason to think you do.'

Fifteen years earlier I'd been angry at Dumisa for partnering with Ed Fagan in the apartheid litigation. Now the shoe was on the other foot and his text opened up wounds that had long since healed. I was furious with Richard, and understood Dumisa's anger. 'I'm very disappointed,' I texted him. 'I cannot associate myself with it and I'm afraid Richard must stand or fall by what he said.'

The hearing continued under strained circumstances, with Richard noticeably absent. I'd rebuked him in private and he'd expressed regret, but he still had to face the music. On the last day of the hearing, Dumisa and Advocate Dali Mpofu led more than one hundred black advocates to court to express their disapproval of Richard's remarks. After seeking the court's permission, they were allowed to read out a memorandum condemning Richard's racist rant:

> We reject these blanket and unwarranted attacks on us and other black colleagues as untrue and motivated by the kind of racial bigotry and prejudice which is inimical to and in gross violation of the spirit and letter of our democratic Constitution … This intervention will hopefully spark the necessary debate on the racism in our profession, which affects both internal and many external role players.

As I listened to the statement, I felt morally compromised and I wondered if I should have taken a public stance against Richard. Yet I knew the good in him and his commitment to human-rights work. Had I made the right call? I reserved my judgment.

—◊—

If astrology has any truth to it, then 13 May 2016 was already written in the stars – the zodiac was in Taurus on that day, symbolising strength, confidence and abundance. That's what I felt when I walked into a packed courtroom on judgment day, accompanied by one of Hausfeld's lawyers. In the public gallery were some former mineworkers in a buoyant mood, anticipating what was to come. Vuyani Dwadube, one of the lead claimants, looked at me with an optimistic smile. I smiled back. Silence fell as the judges entered. Then came the judgment:

The scope and magnitude of the proposed silicosis and TB claims is unprecedented in South Africa. The action, if it proceeds, will entail and traverse novel and complex issues both of fact and law ... The mineworkers have urged the court to consider that, in the context of this case, there is, for most victims of silicosis and tuberculosis, no realistic alternative to class action.

I found it hard to contain my emotion as Judge Phineas Mojapelo read:

We have to assume, for present purposes, that the mining companies have violated [the gold miners'] constitutional, statutory and common law rights as at this stage the mineworkers have made out a prima facie case in this regard.

Then came the part I'd been waiting for:

We have to hold the view that in the context of this case class action is the only realistic option through which most mineworkers can assert their claims effectively against the mining companies. This is the only avenue to realise the right of access to the courts which is guaranteed for them by the Constitution.

The courtroom exploded in jubilation and the miners' faces radiated joy. It took a moment for me to realise the enormity of the judgment. Tens of thousands of miners had been given the green light to proceed with a class action against South Africa's gold-mining industry. The courtroom was abuzz with journalists scurrying for comment. As I made my way through the crowd of well-wishers, one of the mining companies' lawyers congratulated me: 'Well done. The day belongs to you.' I thanked her, but the day belonged to the miners.

—⚏—

The gold-mining companies had long known that the writing was on the wall. Before the hearing, they'd already enlisted John Brand, one of

South Africa's most respected mediators, and seasoned in-house mining lawyer Michael Schottler to undertake confidential negotiations. Their brief was to find an amicable resolution to the class action, and we seized the opportunity. It resulted in more than two years of protracted negotiations, concluding with a settlement in May 2018. The mining companies agreed to establish a multibillion-rand trust fund (with a minimum guarantee of R5 billion) to compensate miners afflicted with silicosis and tuberculosis. I couldn't have asked for a better outcome. It was a major milestone in my legal career.

For the surviving miners and their family members, however, the settlement could never repair the damage caused by South Africa's gold-mining industry. It offered only a tiny taste of the mountains of meat once promised at Malamulela at Mlamlankuzi, the place of the Hairy-Jaw. Nevertheless, it was a bold measure at redressing the legacy left by despicable specimens such as Cecil John Rhodes.

30

Our prophetic task

When Father Henry gifted me fifty rand to spend on first-year law textbooks, he advised me that 'Law should be in service of the public and not only the self.' Thus, I've wrought social change through and with the law as best I could. The few legal successes I've achieved represent what I set out to do, and for that reason I can look back on them with pride. However, in many respects, I've also failed. As incredible a tool as law is, it's also stubbornly static, lacking innovation and energy when it comes to changing society. More often, it's a blunt instrument that leads to arbitrary outcomes. Nowhere was that more evident than in the decade-long Khulumani litigation in the US.

However, anyone with an enduring belief in the possibility of another world and a commitment to making it a reality needs to regularly assess the adequacy of their tools and the means by which they seek to rework society. For me, that opportunity came in February 2010, when I visited Harvard University at the invitation of its law clinic and came across the works of one of its law professors, Roberto Mangabeira Unger. Brazilian by birth, Unger spent most of his life immersed in both theoretical and practical political projects that could serve as alternatives to the current sociopolitical and economic models prevalent around the world.

In contrast to my belief in law as a tool for effecting social change, Unger argues that

> law is best understood as the institutional form of the life of a people, viewed in relation to the interests and ideals that make sense – to its own participants – of that form of life. Our interests and ideals

always remain nailed to the cross of the practices and institutions that represent them as fact. Law is the site of this crucifixion.

I understood Unger to mean that law was a terrain of contest for the ideals and interests of a society. Battles are fought over it and sacrifices made. In the end, law either represents the values of the victors or becomes an amalgam of disparate interests.

Even more interesting were Unger's views on humanity's longing for a larger life:

> The world remains restless [and] has not despaired of finding a better way to fulfil the central promise of democracy, which is to acknowledge and to equip the constructive genius of ordinary men and women. The ambition motivating this search is not merely a desire for a greater equality; it is the demand for a larger life. Such a life must grant people more than a modest prosperity and independence, and more than relief from the extremes of poverty, drudgery, and oppression ... It must offer as well an ascent towards the experience of self-possession and self-making

These thoughts reinvigorated my revolutionary bliss, which had begun to founder. I had pursued most of my cases with vigour, but the practice of law had too often strangled me in mundane legal rules and practices. As a result, I sometimes viewed law as a technical vocation less useful than law as a tool for social change. Unger's view allowed me to regain perspective of law's greater vocation as the tapestry upon which a society's ideals and values are pinned. Even though I regarded law as a tool, Unger's views confirmed what I'd set out to achieve with many of the cases I took on – demonstrating the ways in which law intersects and contrasts with politics, economics and social life in general.

What enlivened me about Unger was his idea of a larger life for ordinary men and women, that our struggle is not only for greater equality but for a larger share of our humanity; an enhancement of our individual agency. The goal of empowerment, he argues, is 'to lift the burden of infirmity, drudgery, and weakness, of incapacity and indignity, that continues to lie so heavily on mankind; to seek light in the shadowy world of the commonplace; to give practical effect to the central teaching of democracy, the doctrine of the greatness of ordinary men and women.'

If, as Unger suggests, democracy is premised on a belief in the greatness and intelligence of ordinary people, and promises to equip their 'constructive genius', then apartheid's chief ambition, in contrast, was to insult, disarm and strangle the intelligence of ordinary black people. Looking at my family, its impact is still visible. After my mother's death, Roseline took charge of the household and cared for my ageing father while running a little crèche from the Bream Way home. She too had dreams of studying further, but put them on hold. After being taken out of school to care for our younger siblings, Mara never received any further formal schooling. She still lives in the vaal flats, but remains hopeful of one day living somewhere else. She has left it to God to decide.

Amanda moved into a support facility with other mental patients and since then has not had any further psychotic episodes. Ronel fell pregnant at an early age and a failed marriage took its toll on her. She too was diagnosed with schizophrenia, but unlike Amanda's psychoses, which were often characterised by anger and rage, Ronel's are peaceful. Her favourite delusion is of being married to Jackie Chan.

Of my other siblings, Marius became a lawyer and Anneline a banker. For Christopher, Lorenzo and Johan, matters went far from well. Despite his wonderful personality, Christopher's life was consumed by alcohol. Lorenzo never recovered from my mother's death. He too suffered from mental illness, and resorted to the bottle. Johan and I remained distant after I fought with him for stealing my clients' money, and I regret never having made amends. On the night of 16 July 2016, Marius called me to tell me that Johan had died. The news ripped through me like a blade. Johan had been in and out of prison, and like so many prisoners, had contracted tuberculosis, which had caused his death.

But Francois's life perplexed me. After his jubilant return from exile, he made Johannesburg his home and was confident that life in the new

South Africa would be filled with promise. I saw the expectation in his eyes: the belief that the city of gold would deliver the struggle dividend he'd invested in. 'Charles, I'm doing a business course,' he'd tell me, excited. 'Please help me with the registration and tuition fees. Once I get my job, I'll pay you back.' I'd dutifully oblige.

Francois registered for one course after the other, but when he applied for work, the disappointments kept coming. 'Sorry, vacancy filled.' 'Sorry, no expertise.' In many instances, he was not even granted a response. He'd remain optimistic nevertheless, saying, I've spoken to so-and-so who promised me this and that and I'm hopeful of landing a job. But nothing ever materialised. Over time, gloom set in and his tone darkened. He would refuse to speak about the struggle years, and his life became filled with bitterness and regret. 'Why did I join the damn liberation struggle? I wasted my entire life,' was a recurring self-accusation. I assured him that things would change, but they didn't. In a final effort, Francois applied for a special struggle veteran's pension, but that was also turned down. Perhaps his misfortune stemmed from having backed the wrong liberation movement. Maybe if he had been ANC and not PAC, things would have been different.

It was his silence about his high-school arch-rival, Francois Groepe, that spoke the loudest. My brother had represented the group who believed in liberation before the detestable Bantu education. Groepe had believed in education before liberation, and had gone on to become a deputy governor of the South African Reserve Bank. Years of rejection broke my brother's liberation spirit and he retreated into a world of religion.

—⟋⟍—

The story of my family resembles the stories of myriad families struggling in post-apartheid South Africa, for whom a larger life remains elusive. For some, life changed, but for many it stayed the same. I've heard some argue that this is the logic of change, whether radical or trivial. I disagree with this cynical view that change only ever benefits a few. Of the many 'freedom' documents that sought to crystallise the hopes and expectations of post-apartheid South Africans, the Freedom Charter stood out. What better way to express our dreams than through the dictum that the people shall govern; that they shall share in the country's wealth and the land on which they work; that the doors of learning and culture shall open; that the people shall have work and security and, most importantly, be equal before the law? So spirited were our longings that a name was coined for us – the Rainbow Nation. The term has since become synonymous with South Africa's 'miraculous' post-apartheid transition, and people relish it to this day.

The problem with rainbows is that they are optical illusions. They don't last forever, and neither do hopes and expectations. If democracy does not fulfil the demand for a larger life, misery and despair will set in. More than two decades after the demise of apartheid, this is exactly what has happened. We need only look around to see that our buoyant spirits have dissipated and the rainbow has all but faded.

In his 1960 novel *No Longer at Ease*, Chinua Achebe provides a glimpse of how hope crumbles when built on faith in a corrupt country. Set in the twilight years of colonial Nigeria, the book tells the story of young Obi Okonkwo, a British-educated Nigerian who returns to Lagos, full of optimism for his country. Obi soon finds himself up against a colonial system entrenched in sleaze and corruption.

When he applies for a job with the Public Service Commission, he is asked if he wants the job so that he can take bribes. Obi considers this an idiotic question, but avoids giving a definite answer. He gets the job, but because the officials around him are corrupt, he too succumbs to corruption. Obi's moral foundations are eventually broken by his burdensome debts and his mother's disapproval of his girlfriend, Clara, an osu (outcast), and the country that he loves is unable to provide the moral support that would strengthen his own integrity and convictions.

Even though Obi's story occurs in colonial Nigeria, I found it relevant to post-apartheid South Africa. Breaking with our colonial past provided no protection from the cancer of corruption, which made a seamless transition into the new South Africa. All it required was willing hosts, and we seemed to have no shortage of those.

Achebe's subsequent novel, *A Man of the People* (1966), vividly demonstrates the cause and impact of corruption. Set in an unnamed post-colonial country, the novel pits Odili Samalu, a highly motivated and sincere teacher, against Chief Nanga, a powerful but corrupt minister of culture who was once Odili's schoolteacher. The novel opens with Odili waiting for Nanga to address the school and its villagers. While waiting, Odili experiences 'intense bitterness' as he observes the villagers:

> Here were silly, ignorant villagers dancing themselves lame and waiting to blow off their gunpowder in honour of one of those who had started the country off down the slopes of inflation. I wished for a miracle, for a voice of thunder, to hush this ridiculous festival and tell the poor contemptable people one or two truths. But of course it would be quite useless.

Odile's disillusion takes place against the backdrop of his discontent with the politics of his country. The president of the governing political party, the People's Organisation Party (POP), of which he and Nanga were members, had sacked the highly respected and well-educated minister of finance after disagreeing with the minister's plan for dealing with the country's economic crisis. As a cover for his action, the president, in Parliament, accused him and other ministers (also sacked as conspirators and traitors) of being a 'Miscreant Gang' who had teamed up with foreign saboteurs to overthrow the government and destroy their new nation. To which Nanga shouted, 'They deserve to be hanged.'

Achebe wanted us to understand that independence, instead of fulfilling the central promise of democracy, can become the proxy through which an old, corrupt colonial elite is replaced by an equally corrupt local, African elite. This point is aptly made by Odili's observation of Nanga's opulent lifestyle when he visits his home.

> A man who has just come in from the rain and dried his body and put on dry clothes is more reluctant to go out again than another

who has been indoors all the time. The trouble with our new nation
... was that none of us had been indoors long enough to be able
to say 'To hell with it'. We had all been in the rain together until
yesterday. Then a handful of us – the smart and the lucky and
hardly ever the best – had scrambled for the one shelter our former
rulers left, and had taken it over and barricaded themselves in.

More sordid is the manner in which Nanga and other corrupt leaders
use ordinary men and women to achieve their nefarious ends, to the
point where they too condone corruption. As the villagers dance while
waiting for Nanga, Odili reflects: 'Tell them that this man had used his
position to enrich himself and they would ask you ... if you thought
that a sensible man would spit out the juicy morsel that good fortune
placed in his mouth?'

Achebe's two novels suggest that, in order for the majority to benefit
from change, independence must be truly transformative. I believe that
true independence and genuine diversity – not just rainbow metaphors
– only have meaning if they dare to confront the systemic vestiges and
entrenched corruption of colonialism and apartheid. This is not only
a social concern, but demands that we personally assess our beliefs,
from our most intimate social, cultural and religious views and practices to the political, economic and ideological ideals and institutions
we put our faith in. Everything should be up for scrutiny. In this way,
we'll ensure our post-apartheid ideals and interests, whether expressed
in law, institutions or practices, will provide us with a pathway towards
a larger life for all.

Each discipline in life has transformative power and I've invested in
law's. Law isn't the sole preserve of lawyers, judges and legal academics.
It concerns us all. We all have a stake in it. It is our prophetic task to
use it, not in the future, but in the now.

31

A time to rest and reflect

It's been a long journey from my childhood dream of wanting to be a world-famous heart surgeon to ending up as a lawyer. Occasionally, I wonder how my life might have turned out had I become a surgeon. It's idle speculation, but I take comfort in what Steve Jobs, co-founder of Apple, said: 'you can't connect the dots looking forward; you can only connect them looking backwards. So you have to trust that the dots somehow connect in the future.'

When I look back and connect the dots, I realise how much they hinted at the future. Through law, I sought to mend the social wounds caused by apartheid, and class actions became the scalpel with which I performed those surgeries. In that way, I didn't stray too far from my childhood dream. In addition, I have also sought to heal the damage and brokenness inside of me. These attempts have been haphazard; a patchwork affair.

I look back to Bream Way with enmity and respect. Growing up on that street shaped my life. I witnessed brutal gang wars, ruthless killings and senseless violence. Yet, despite Bream Way being cruel and merciless, it is also a place of cherished memories of children playing carefree, forming endearing friendships, having dreams and showing respect towards adults. Even the gangs occasionally allowed children some measure of slack to be children, by fighting at night rather than during the day. Bream Way truly was and will continue to be a place of contradictions.

But that street also demanded its pound of flesh, and the many psychological wounds I carry bear testimony to that. While a few have healed, others have only had costly cosmetic surgery, and some still ache. My experience at the hands of Uncle Sammy is a case in point. Even though I've long since moved on, his abuse still haunts me. I knew that sooner or later our paths would cross, and they did, in 2016, when a family outing took a detour to Elim. It's a small town, and I unexpectedly bumped into him. Apparently he'd retired there. He was shaken and surprised to see me, unsure of the purpose of my visit. Our conversation was strained. We occasionally made eye contact as I introduced my family to him and he spoke of his. I could sense his discomfort. Even though I did not confront him, I left with a distinct feeling that he knew his time had come; sooner or later he would have to own up to what he'd done.

I've sought to make amends with Simone and Merilyn. After our tumultuous break-up in 2002, Simone and I didn't speak for nearly five years. In 2006, after much heartache and rage had subsided, she broke her silence, and we had a cathartic talk. She even surprised me and Turcia with a visit to Cape Town in 2010, a year after the birth of my second son, Peter. Merilyn and I started to converse, only to find that the emotions between us were still raw.

A few years ago, Francois and I decided to visit mean-spirited Sasman, our former neighbour who had killed Francois's little chicks with a spade. When we arrived at his doorstep, he was so overwhelmed that he said, 'Now I've seen my grace, God can take me away.' We all felt a sense of relief.

Regrettably, there was no sense of relief when I encountered Baartman at a high-school reunion. After learning of my success, he hurried over in excitement to greet me, clearly clueless about the trauma he'd once caused. His face collapsed when I reminded him of the time he'd beaten me and my friends until we could barely walk, for nothing more than dancing in class.

Meanwhile, my father had grown old. In the two decades after my mother's death, he saw what she'd had to endure when he was absent from home. The unsettled lives of my brothers Johan and Lorenzo caused him much grief. The strain it took on him may have caused his health to deteriorate, and in 2017 he was diagnosed with prostate cancer. On 6 June 2018, two years after Johan's death, my father died at the age of eighty-six. Like my mother's funeral, his was a moving affair. One of his early Christian converts testified about my father's evangelical work in the rural town of Ceres. During his many trips there, he had slept in squalor with destitute farmworkers and eaten fly-infested food with them. It was his way of showing his and God's love to them. I became teary and got a sense of where I'd got my concern for the poor, marginalised and indigent from. As much as I abhorred what my father had done to my mother, I realised I wasn't only Ketie's son, but Broer Baard's son too.

—⚭—

I've come a long way from the skinny boy born in a sinkhokkie on the outskirts of Elsies River. I traversed Bream Way's circles of hell and grappled with great philosophers in the City Library. I still experience a sense of frustration with Karl Marx for having written books too complex to be easily understood by working-class readers, who were supposed to be the major benefactors of his ideas. Despite all the studying and research I've done since then, I still haven't finished reading *Capital*. Nevertheless, Marx's ideas have left a profound impression on me. So, too, has religion. Even though I never fully embraced Marxism or completely rejected religion, I'm convinced that somewhere within those domains lie ideas and beliefs that can provide hope for a larger life. But what better way to discover such a life than through our daily experiences?

Despite its contradictions, Bream Way equipped me with the personal qualities to pursue a larger life, to expand my humanity beyond what apartheid had deemed fit for people like me. It tempered me with resilience and dexterity when faced with the unbearable, the dreadful and, at times, the impossible. It made me bold and fearless, qualities I sorely needed to speak and act truth to power and, more importantly, to face myself. Through Bream Way, I discovered who I really was – a deeply flawed person wrought of paradoxes, yet driven by an unfathomable desire for compassion, benevolence and humanity. Bream Way helped me figure out my identity amid the dread and misery of a childhood marred by racism and subjugation. I have long since shed the shame of my coloured identity and discovered the pride and joy of being black and African. But the greatest discovery I made was the realisation that there was more to me than being black and African. Through my pursuit of a larger life, I discovered that race, creed or class alone cannot define my identity or anyone else's. There is much more in each of us than the traits we use to identify ourselves. Through Bream Way, I glimpsed what it means to live a larger life.

—⚏—

When I look at the middle-class life I live now, I am fearful that it will make me complacent and that the knowledge of my connection to a broader humanity will fade. Since I qualified as a lawyer, many have hailed me for having escaped my harsh and impoverished working-class background and made it into material comfort. I'm held up as a success story, a role-model or poster-boy for having overcome the odds. I've graciously accepted these well-meaning accolades but struggle to understand what is meant by 'made it': where have I made it to? I shudder at the thought that I've entered a world that admits very few while the rest remain excluded, condemned to lives tightly constrained by poverty and lack.

During one of my trips to New York to attend a court hearing on the Khulumani class action, I received a frantic call from my sister Amanda in Cape Town. 'Charles! Charles! Where are you?' she yelled, hysterical. Before I could respond, she summoned me to the family home in Nooitgedacht. I was afraid that Amanda was about to have a psychotic breakdown even though she hadn't had one in years. When I told her I was in New York, she asked, 'New York? Where's New York?'

'In America,' I told her.

'Oh! America.' And then she slammed the phone down.

It turned out that a minor squabble among my brothers had upset her. Amanda's call was a sobering reminder that, despite my having made it, my family's troubles still haunted me. I was seen as the strong one, the go-to person to fix their problems, and those problems followed me wherever I went. But her call also reminded me that many people remain trapped in lives so infinitely removed from the world as epitomised by New York. Here I was, having navigated the odds, in this global powerhouse of a city, working on an international lawsuit I'd set in motion, while Amanda was stuck in Nooitgedacht where my family bickered without the means to resolve their problems on their own. At the same time, I was aware of how the glamorous sophistication of cities like New York rested on the backs of people who would never know about it. Amanda had thrown these connections into sharp relief.

I've realised that, far from having made it, I've only arrived at a resting place with the resources to refuel, take stock and prepare for ongoing activism. To look at it otherwise, to see my middle-class life as an end goal, may render me complicit in a world that's happy to welcome a few like me into the fold while condemning the many, Amanda among them. If she has to ask, 'Where's New York?' then heaven forbid that I should one day find myself asking, 'Where is Nooitgedacht?'

References

p. 27   'a cry, a very loud cry ...': Joseph Conrad, *Heart of Darkness* (New York: Penguin Books, 2017), p. 78

p. 41   'Through me you pass into the city of woe ...': Dante Alighieri, *The Divine Comedy*, tr. H.F. Cary (eBooks@Adelaide, 2014), https://ebooks.adelaide.edu.au/d/dante/d19he/canto3.html, last accessed October 2018

p. 50   'Perhaps the greatest crime ...': Jane Gool, *The Crimes of Bantu Education* (South Africa: Unity Movement Publication, 1966), p. 1, http://www.apdusa.org.za/wp-content/books/crimes.of.bantu.education.pdf, last accessed October 2018

p. 50   'Thus the African child ...': ibid.

p. 65   'The wealth of societies ...': Karl Marx, *Capital: Volume 1*, tr. Ben Fowkes and D. Fernbach (London: Penguin Books, 1976), p. 125

p. 68   'Religious suffering is, at one and the same time ...': Karl Marx, *Critique of Hegel's Philosophy of Right*, tr. Annette Jolin and Joseph O'Malley (Cambridge University Press, 1970), p. 131

p. 69   'Our history is the greatest masterpiece of the centuries ...': D.F. Malan, as quoted by T. Dunbar Moodie in *The Rise of Afrikanerdom* (University of California Press, 1975), p. 1

p. 70   'international finance served as the main link ...': Karl Polanyi, *The Great Transformation* (Boston, Massachusetts: Beacon Press, 2001), p. 10–11

p. 71   'I know very well ...': Adolf Hitler, as quoted by Neville Alexander in *Sow the Wind* (Johannesburg: Skotaville Publishers, 1985), p. 144

p. 72   'Today, from now on, there is a new African in the world ...': Kwame Nkrumah in *Africa and the West: A documentary history*, eds William

H. Worger, Nancy L. Clark and Edward A. Alpers (New York: Oxford University Press, 2010), vol. 2, p.128

p. 72 'Xhosas want their Transkei …': Steve Biko, *I Write What I Like* (University of Chicago Press, 1978), p.36

p. 73 'Coloured people harbour secret hopes …': ibid.

p. 73 '[E]very colonized people …': Frantz Fanon, *Black Skin, White Masks*, tr. Charles Lam Markmann, revised ed. (London: Pluto Press, 2008), p. 9

p. 73 'The black man who has lived in France …': ibid., p. 10

p. 74 'Because it is a systematic negation …': Frantz Fanon, *The Wretched of the Earth*, tr. Constance Farrington (New York: Grove Press, 1963), p. 250

p. 140 'The salvation of man …': Viktor E. Frankl, *Man's Search for Meaning*, tr. Ilse Lasch (London: Rider, 2008), p. 49

p. 142 'The majority of them …': Frantz Fanon, *Black Skin, White Masks*, p. 50

p. 142 'I wonder whether …': ibid.

p. 154 'The *National Law Journal* named him …': Michael Hausfeld bio, http://michaelhausfeld.com/, last accessed October 2018

p. 159 'The bank regards the subscription': Bob Aldworth, as quoted by Terry Shott in 'The banks and the military in South Africa', at the International Seminar on Loans to South Africa, 5–7 April 1981

p. 163 'You people have not been trained …': John E. Sprizzo, as quoted by William Glaberson in 'The law; Judge refuses to open proceedings', *New York Times*, 10 March 1989, https://www.nytimes.com/1989/03/10/nyregion/the-law-judge-refuses-to-open-proceeding.html, last accessed October 2018

p. 183 'I contend that we are the finest race in the world …': Cecil John Rhodes, 'Confession of Faith' (1877), https://pages.uoregon.edu/kimball/Rhodes-Confession.htm, last accessed October 2018

p. 184 'When the recruiters invaded our homes …': Alfred Temba Qabula, *A Working Life, Cruel Beyond Belief* (Johannesburg: National Union of Metalworkers of South Africa, 1989), p. 51

p. 188 'Words strain …', T.S. Eliot, 'Burnt Norton' (1936), with permission from Faber & Faber Ltd and HMH Trade Publishing

p. 192 '[W]hy no black counsel …': Richard Spoor on Facebook, as screen-shotted by Kevin Malunga, 18 October 2015, https://twitter.com/KevinMalunga/status/655632587650682880, last accessed December 2018

p. 193 'We reject these blanket and unwarranted attacks …': Advocates for Transformation, 'Black advocates tell court they object to "racist sting"', *GroundUp*, 23 October 2015, https://www.groundup.org.za/article/black-advocates-object-racist-sting-court_3430/, last accessed December 2018

p. 194 'The scope and magnitude …': Southern African Legal Information Institute, *Nkala and Others v Harmony Gold Mining Company Limited and Others*, 13 May 2016, http://www.saflii.org/za/cases/ZAGP-JHC/2016/97.html, last accessed December 2018

p. 194 'We have to assume …': ibid.

p. 194 'We have to hold the view …': ibid.

p. 197 'law is best understood …' Roberto Mangabeira Unger, 'The universal history of legal thought', p. 48, http://www.robertounger.com/en/wp-content/uploads/2017/01/the-universal-history-of-legal-thought.pdf, last accessed October 2018

p. 198 '[t]he world remains restless …': Roberto Mangabeira Unger, *The Left Alternative* (New York: Verso, 2009), p. vii

p. 198 'to lift the burden of infirmity …': Roberto Mangabeira Unger, *False Necessity: Anti-necessitarian Social Theory in the Service of Radical Democracy* (London: Verso, 2004), p. xix

p. 202 'Here were silly, ignorant villagers …': Chinua Achebe, *A Man of the People* (Nairobi: East African Educational Publishers, 2004), p. 2

p. 202 'They deserve to be hanged', ibid., p. 5

p. 202 'A man who has just come in from the rain …', ibid., p. 37

p. 203 'Tell them that this man …': ibid., p. 2

p. 205 'you can't connect the dots …': Steve Jobs, 'Commencement address', *Stanford News*, 14 June 2005, https://news.stanford.edu/2005/06/14/jobs-061505/, last accessed December 2018